THE BEST OF
CHINA

THE BEST OF
CHINA
A COOKBOOK

Evie Righter

Recipes by Grace Wiertz Young
Food Photography by Steven Mark Needham

CollinsPublishersSanFrancisco
A Division of HarperCollinsPublishers

First published in USA 1992 by Collins Publishers San Francisco

Produced by Smallwood and Stewart Inc.,
New York City

© 1992 Smallwood and Stewart, Inc.

Edited by Alice Wong
Jacket design by Nina Ovryn   Book design by Dianna Russo
Food styling by Ann Disrude   Prop styling by Betty Alfenito

Photography credits: Charles Bowman/Picture Perfect: 1; 2-3; 49.
Jim Brandenburg/Minden Pictures: 67. Jean S. Buldain/Picture Perfect:
7; 25. E.R. Degginger/Picture Perfect: 33; 61. Frans Lanting/Minden
Pictures: 13; 37. R. Thompson/Picture Perfect: 79; 85.

Library of Congress Cataloging-in-Publication Data

Righter, Evie
    The Best of China: a cookbook/Evie Righter;
recipes by Grace Young.
        p. cm.
    Includes index.
    ISBN 0-00-255149-7; $14.95
    1. Cookery, Chinese.   I. Title.
TX724.5.C5R54   1992
641.5951—dc20   92-17592
                                          CIP

Printed in Hong Kong

Contents

Introduction

We recognize the words, and sometimes even the different spellings ~ Peking/Beijing, Szechwan/Sichuan, Hunan, Shanghai, Canton ~ and we know where we are. Or do we? China is the third-largest and most-populated country in the world, where the climate veers from near-arctic in the north, in Mongolia, to subtropical in the south along beaches washed by the South China Sea. In China, the language consists not of letters, but of magnificent ideograms lyrically formed with ink and brush.

For the Westerner, there is perhaps only one certainty when it comes to things Chinese: What greets the eye in this complicated, sophisticated, millenia-old culture is never all there is. Something else, another meaning, always awaits. Nothing in China is as it seems, right down to and including its compelling, completely tantalizing cuisine.

Centuries ago, the Chinese divided their food into two major classifications: *fan*, encompassing rice, other grains, breads, and noodles; and *tsai*, including meat, poultry, seafood, and vegetable dishes that act to enhance *fan*. A well-conceived Chinese meal, from the simplest to the

A Chinese junk on the Yangtze River

most elaborate, should effortlessly unite *fan* with accompaniments from *tsai*, and that is only the first, and probably the most straightforward, requisite. Add to it the basic Chinese tenet that there are five fundamental flavors ~ sweet, sour, salty, bitter, and spicy ~ and that contrast in these is one of the goals in a successful combination of Chinese dishes, too.

Most important though, there is the philosophic principle of *yin-yang* that underscores all Chinese life, including its cuisine. Food is believed to have *yin* or cold properties, also sometimes described as dark and feminine, and *yang* or hot properties, conversely described as bright and masculine, and these affect the body. Harmony is everything, but to balance the juxtaposition of opposites is the ultimate goal.

In sum, the selection of dishes in a Chinese meal is meant to contrast as well as harmonize. Flavors complement but play off each other. Specific ingredients are there to please, but also to cleanse, rid, and cure the system of known or suspected impurities. And none of this even takes into account that cooking techniques ~ stir-frying, braising, steaming, deep-frying, dry-frying ~ are also meant to be varied.

As with other great cuisines, geography and climate have played their part on the cooking of China, but no more so than the ingenuity and creativeness of the Chinese spirit, a spirit thousands of years old. The marvelous noodle preparations, dumplings, and breads hail from the north, land of wheat. Here we find Beijing, where at one time in the Forbidden City banquets were celebrated over a period of several days. Inland and west are the provinces of Sichuan and Hunan, each acclaimed for its hot and spicy dishes, but where, interestingly, the food is still subtly seasoned. South on the coast, most notably Canton, stir-frying reigns for diverse but simply prepared recipes, and seasonings like fermented black beans lend their magic to mild-flavored dishes of fish and chicken. On the bounteous central coast, Yangzhou, Wuxi, and Shanghai are among the cities of eastern China famed for their succulent and flavorful creations.

Grace Young, whose recipes fill this book with a small sampling of the innumerable pleasures of Chinese cooking, once described how the cook in China washes vegetables. She washes them early in the morning, carefully, patiently, tirelessly, then leaves them out to dry until needed. Day in and day out, this is the custom. That is how I would suggest using this book ~ day in and day out, as a way of cooking to be enjoyed and explored, then enjoyed and explored some more, over the course of a lifetime.

Evie Righter

Equipment and Techniques

The wok: The essential piece of cooking equipment in a Chinese kitchen is the wok. This large, rounded, metal pan has sloped sides and a relatively small cooking surface for the most efficient use of heat. Of the various types and sizes of woks, we recommend the slope-sided wok (about 14 inches across the top) with a flat bottom. Unlike the round-bottom wok, no ring is needed to balance it. Stir-frying, deep-frying, and steaming can be undertaken safely and easily, with the maximum amount of heat directed to the bottom of the pan.

A new wok must be cleaned according to the manufacturer's instructions, in warm water with soap and an abrasive cleanser to remove the machine oil used to protect the metal surface in shipping. Season the wok with oil after the first washing and after the first few uses to prepare its surface and to prevent rusting. To season, dry the wok thoroughly, then heat it over the burner until hot but not smoking. Soak a double thickness of paper towels with vegetable oil, then rub the entire surface of the inside of the wok with the oil. The oil will sink in and the wok will start to darken. Let the wok cool and wipe off the excess oil.

Clean a wok out immediately after use, while it is still hot from cooking, with hot water and a sponge or scrub brush. Do not use soap and never an abrasive. Should food stick, rub if off with a brush. Do not let a wok soak with water in it. Dry the cleaned-out wok thoroughly.

The Chinese cleaver: This is the tool for shredding, chopping, smashing, and cutting of all kinds. With a square blade and strong handle, the cleaver, available in various weights, is a most serious utensil, best washed immediately after use and put away in a safe cabinet. A well-sharpened knife makes a very good substitute.

Stir-frying: In a wok over medium-high or high heat, food is tossed with a metal spatula so that all surfaces of the food touch the hot wok without resting in any one spot and overcooking. To stir-fry "rapidly" is to keep the contents of the wok in constant, fluid motion. Always scoop from the bottom of the wok up, turning the food over completely but gently.

Deep-frying: For the very best results, heat the oil to the temperature given in the recipe. Carefully add the ingredients to be deep-fried to the hot oil and remember that the slightest amount of water will cause the hot oil to splatter fiercely. Turn food that is deep-frying with a slotted spoon or a pair of bamboo chopsticks, and when done, transfer it to paper towels to drain. Allow the oil to reheat fully before adding the next batch of food.

Steaming: The benefits of steamed food are many ~ the preservation of essential, sweet flavors; the retention of moisture; and the ease of preparation. Thanks to Chinese invention, we have the bamboo steamer: covered woven baskets that stack upon each other and fit into a wok over boiling water. To improvise a steamer, place a rack or metal trivet in the bottom of a wok and put the food to be steamed on a plate on the rack. Add an inch or two of water to the wok, cover, and steam as directed. Open the lid away from you, to prevent steam from flying into your face.

The Recipes

As simple as the most basic Chinese recipe may appear, it is essential to have all the ingredients prepared in advance of cooking. The last-minute chopping of a vegetable, for example, while ingredients overheat in a hot wok, can mean the demise of a wonderful combination. Finally, all ingredients and cookware, unless specified otherwise, should be medium in size.

手撕鷄

Hand-Shredded Chicken Salad with Bean Thread Noodles

This dish typifies the harmony that can derive from contrast: crisp noodles and warm chicken with a tangy but sweet sauce on a bed of crunchy, cool lettuce. The flavors and textures are multiple; the effect superb. Salt-roasted chicken, with the juice in a separate container, can be found in Chinatown markets. If you cannot find salt-roasted chicken, Lemon Chicken (p. 14) is a fine substitute. The chicken should be warm, and more important, the skin crisp. Plain cooked chicken is not an acceptable substitute.

2 cups peanut oil

½ cup raw, shelled, & skinned peanuts

2 ounces bean thread noodles

6 cups shredded iceberg or romaine lettuce

1½ pounds Chinese salt-roasted chicken or Lemon Chicken (p. 14)

3 scallions, finely shredded

2 teaspoons dry mustard

1 tablespoon water

2 teaspoons plus ¼ cup hoisin sauce

¼ cup Chinese salt-roasted chicken juice or Chicken Stock (p. 83)

Coriander sprigs for garnish

Heat the oil in a wok over high heat to 375°F. With a slotted spoon, carefully add peanuts and fry for 30 seconds to 1 minute, or until golden brown. Remove peanuts to paper towels to drain, then crush them with the back of a cleaver.

Return the oil in the wok to 375°F. and carefully add the bean threads. (They will puff up immediately upon contact with the oil.) Deep fry no more than 5 to 10 seconds.

The famed scenic beauty of Guilin

Once puffed, remove to paper towels to drain and cool.

Line a platter with the lettuce. Lightly crush the noodles and place them on lettuce. Shred the chicken by hand, including the skin, and place in a bowl. Add the scallions. Dissolve the mustard in the water and combine with 2 teaspoons hoisin sauce. Add the mustard-hoisin sauce with the juice or stock to chicken and toss.

Arrange chicken on the platter and sprinkle with peanuts. Garnish with coriander and serve with a small bowl of the remaining hoisin sauce. Serves 4 to 6 as part of a multi-course meal.

檸檬鷄

L e m o n   C h i c k e n

This Cantonese-style chicken is crunchy on the outside, but tender within. It is sweet to the taste, but refreshingly tart when sauced. Be sure to serve it while it is still hot and and the skin is still crispy. If preferred, it can also be prepared with boneless chicken breasts.

2 small chicken breasts with bone & skin, about 2 pounds, washed, patted dry, & halved

2 tablespoons rice wine

2 tablespoons plus 2 teaspoons soy sauce

1 teaspoon plus 2 tablespoons sugar

1 teaspoon salt

½ cup all-purpose flour

2 tablespoons plus 4 teaspoons cornstarch

½ teaspoon baking powder

½ cup cold water

¾ cup Chicken Stock (p. 83)

⅓ cup fresh lemon juice

1 tablespoon plus 5 cups peanut oil

1 tablespoon finely minced garlic

⅓ cup finely minced scallions

2 cups shredded romaine lettuce

Coriander sprigs for garnish

In a large bowl combine well the chicken, wine, 2 tablespoons soy, 1 teaspoon sugar, and salt. Set aside and stir occasionally.

In a bowl combine well the flour, 2 tablespoons cornstarch, baking powder, and water. In another bowl combine the stock, juice,

remaining soy, sugar, and cornstarch.

In a skillet heat 1 tablespoon oil until hot but not smoking and add the garlic and scallions. Stir-fry rapidly until just fragrant. Restir the flour-cornstarch mixture and add to skillet. Cook, stirring, for 1 to 2 minutes, or

until slightly thickened. Remove from heat.

Drain the chicken and pat dry with paper towels. Add chicken to batter and mix until thoroughly coated. Heat 5 cups oil in a wok over medium-high heat to 375°F. With a slotted spoon, carefully add chicken and cook 6 to 10 minutes per side, or until rich golden brown and cooked through. Remove with a spoon to a plate lined with paper towels to drain. Let cool for 5 minutes.

Line a platter with the lettuce. Using a cleaver, cut the chicken through the bone into ½-inch pieces. Arrange on platter and garnish with coriander. Serve with the lemon sauce on the side. Serves 4 to 6 as part of a multi-course meal.

宮保鷄丁

Kung Pao Chicken

This renowned stir-fry from western China combines the flavors of hot dried peppers and fresh bell peppers with the crunch of quickly deep-fried peanuts. Thanks to the sweet hoisin-based sauce, this dish is hot without being fiery. This is classic Chinese cooking at its best, perfectly balanced even in its magnificent assortment of colors.

1½ pounds boneless & skinless chicken, cut into ½-inch cubes

1 tablespoon soy sauce

1 tablespoon rice wine

1 tablespoon cornstarch

1 teaspoon sesame oil

½ cup peanut oil

1 cup raw, shelled, & skinned peanuts

3 slices ginger

4 garlic cloves, lightly smashed & peeled

5 dried red chili peppers

2 large red bell peppers, cut into 1-inch chunks

2 tablespoons hoisin sauce

1 teaspoon red rice vinegar

½ teaspoon sugar

⅓ cup minced scallions

In a bowl combine well the chicken, soy, wine, and cornstarch. Stir in the sesame oil.

Heat the oil in a wok over medium-high heat to 375°F. With a slotted spoon, carefully add the peanuts and fry for 30 seconds to 1 minute, or until golden brown. Remove to a plate lined with paper towels to drain.

Carefully add the ginger, garlic, and dried peppers to the hot oil and fry until they are charred. With a slotted spoon, remove and discard the solid ingredients.

Restir the chicken mixture and carefully add half of it to the hot oil, spreading it in the wok. Cook for 3 to 4 minutes, or until

golden brown. Do not stir, but turn occasionally. Remove to a plate and repeat with remaining chicken.

Remove all but 1 tablespoon of oil from the wok. Add the bell peppers and stir-fry rapidly for 1 to 2 minutes, or until peppers begin to soften. Return the chicken to the wok, add the hoisin sauce, vinegar, and sugar and stir-fry rapidly for 1 minute or until heated through. Add the peanuts and scallions and stir-fry rapidly for 30 seconds until scallions are bright green. Serve immediately. Serves 4 to 6 as part of a multi-course meal.

茶葉燻鷄

Tea-Smoked Chicken

It is hard to believe that any chicken can be steamed, and then smoked, and turn out the way it does here ~ burnished mahogany in color, magnificently aromatic, and flavored with cinnamon, star anise, and tea. For the very best results, allow yourself sufficient time: The recipe, which is popular in the north and west of China, is done over a two-day period. Do not be daunted by the amount of smoke that billows forth during smoking; that is the sign and the smell that the process is working. Do, though, throw the smoking combination out immediately after cooking to prevent the aromas from completely settling into your home.

10 cups water

3 tablespoons soy sauce

½ cup rice wine

2 tablespoons salt

1 tablespoon sesame oil

1 tablespoon Sichuan peppercorns

One 1-inch piece ginger

One 2-inch piece cinnamon stick

1 star anise

One 3½-pound fresh chicken, excess fat removed, & washed

Smoking Ingredients:

1 cup dry black tea leaves

1 cup long-grain rice

½ cup light or dark brown sugar

1 tablespoon Sichuan peppercorns

4 pieces dried orange peel

One 2-inch piece cinnamon stick

2 star anise

In a large pot bring the water, soy, wine, salt, oil, peppercorns, ginger, cinnamon, and star anise to a boil over medium-high heat. Reduce heat to low, and simmer uncovered for 10 minutes. Let cool completely. Add the chicken to the pot, breast side down, and cover pot. Refrigerate for 24 hours.

Remove the chicken from the liquid and place it in a shallow heatproof bowl large enough to fit into a bamboo steamer. Place dish in steamer and cover steamer with bamboo lid. Bring 3 cups of water to a boil in a covered wok. Place covered steamer in wok, and steam chicken for 45 minutes, about 15 minutes per pound, checking the water level and replenishing it, if necessary.

Turn off heat and carefully remove the chicken from the steamer. Place chicken on an oiled metal rack. Remove the liquid in the cavity and combine it with the liquid that has accumulated in the bowl used for steaming. Reserve for serving.

In a large bowl, combine the smoking ingredients. Line a 14-inch wok with 3 layers of heavy-duty aluminum foil with a 3- to 4-inch overhang. Pour the tea mixture into the bottom of wok and set the metal rack with chicken on it over the mixture. (The rack should be 2 inches above the mixture.) Turn on the exhaust fan on the stove, or open the windows to create cross-ventilation. Turn the heat to high. Do not walk away from the stove as the smoking process requires careful monitoring. Watch the tea mixture and in 3 to 4 minutes it will begin to smoke. Cover wok with the lid. Crimp the foil overhang snugly against the lid and smoke chicken for 10 minutes. (If necessary, wearing oven mitts, crimp the foil even more tightly in areas where smoke is escaping.) After 10 minutes, turn off the heat and allow wok to rest for 5 minutes.

Carefully remove the lid, opening it away from your face. If the chicken is light golden brown, smoke it for 10 minutes more. If it is already dark, smoke it for 5 minutes more. To do so, heat the wok, uncovered, for 3 to 4

minutes, or until there is smoke. Cover with the lid, crimp the foil, and smoke chicken until it is the color of mahogany. Turn off the heat and let rest 10 minutes. Carefully remove the lid and transfer chicken to a platter. When the tea mixture is cool enough to handle, wrap it in the foil and discard.

Cut the chicken into serving pieces and serve it with the reserved cooking liquid warm or at room temperature. Serves 4 to 6 as part of a multi-course meal.

燒鴨

C r i s p y   R o a s t   D u c k

This duck recipe from southern China involves a two-step preparation.
First the duck is air-dried, actually left out at room temperature for several
hours as a prelude to crisping the skin. Then the bird is roasted at different
temperatures for about one hour. The result: a beautifully burnished, almost
glossy, crisp-skinned duck. Do not attempt air-drying on a hot, humid day, or even
on a cold winter day when the heating is turned up. The duck should dry in a
well-ventilated, cool place. Some experts recommend putting it in front
of an electric fan. Not incidentally, the juice from the cooked duck, full of the
aromas of ginger, scallion, and garlic, makes the perfect and only sauce needed.
Note: The typical Chinese recipe begins with a duck that still has its head.
The belief is that a whole bird has a fuller flavor. For most American
cooks, it is simply not possible to find a whole duck.

1 teaspoon peanut oil

4 whole scallions plus brushes
    for garnish

4 slices ginger

4 garlic cloves, smashed & peeled

2 tablespoons bean sauce

1 tablespoon dark soy sauce

1 tablespoon soy sauce

1 tablespoon rice wine

2 teaspoons sugar

1 teaspoon Sichuan peppercorns,
    dry roasted & ground

¼ cup packed coriander leaves
    plus additional for garnish

One 4- to 4 ½-pound duck,
    washed

1 tablespoon honey

¼ cup boiling water

Heat a wok over high heat until it is hot. Add the oil, scallions, ginger, and garlic, and stir-fry rapidly for 1 minute, or until fragrant. Add the bean sauce, both soy sauces, wine, sugar, peppercorns, and ¼ cup coriander. Bring to a boil, reduce heat to low, and simmer covered for 5 minutes. Uncover and let cool.

Dry the duck thoroughly with paper towels. Remove the gizzards, neck, and liver, and any visible fat. Dissolve the honey in the boiling water and let cool.

When the scallion-soy mixture has cooled, place the duck on a roasting rack, breast side up, and carefully spoon the cooled mixture into the cavity of the duck through the tail end. Close the end with a bamboo skewer, "stitching" the skewer between the two open ends, and tuck in the tail end. With a pastry brush, brush entire duck lightly with the cooled honey water. (Do not forget the underside of the duck.) Let duck air-dry for 4 to 5 hours, or until skin feels dry and is not even slightly moist to the touch.

Preheat oven to 450°F. Line a large roasting pan with several sheets of heavy-duty aluminum foil. Set the rack with the duck in the pan. Add water to the pan to a depth of ¼ inch. Roast duck for 20 minutes. Reduce oven temperature to 350°F. and roast for 20 minutes more. Check duck. If any part of it is browning too much, cover with a patch of aluminum foil. Roast an additional 15 to 20 minutes, or until duck is a rich brown color and is cooked through.

Carefully remove the duck to a platter. Remove the skewer and the solids in the cavity, and carefully pour the juice from the cavity into a bowl. Skim the fat from the juice.

Cut the duck into serving pieces and garnish with scallion brushes and coriander leaves. Serve immediately, while skin is crisp, with the warm juice as a sauce. Serves 4 to 6 as part of a multi-course meal.

叉燒

R o a s t P o r k

While many Chinese cooks will go to the market for this barbecue pork,
a featured ingredient in Steamed Roast Pork Buns (p. 74) and to a lesser extent in
Spring Rolls (p. 76), making it at home is not difficult. Served sliced, this flavorful
meat is a nice addition to any meal as well as a wonderful snack for nibbling.
Pork butt is called for. If you wish a less fatty cut, use the loin.

*2 pounds boneless pork butt or
  pork loin, trimmed*

1 tablespoon dark soy sauce

1 tablespoon soy sauce

1 tablespoon hoisin sauce

1 tablespoon bean sauce

1 tablespoon rice wine

2 tablespoons sugar

1 tablespoon finely minced garlic

Cut the pork lengthwise into 1½-inch-wide strips. In a large bowl combine remaining ingredients. Add pork strips and let them marinate covered, in the refrigerator, for 3 to 4 hours. Turn strips every hour to make sure flavors develop evenly.

Set a roasting pan filled with ½ inch water in the bottom of the oven. Remove all the racks in the oven except the top rack. Using clean curved metal skewers (available at Chinese cookware stores), hook each pork strip.

Preheat the oven to 350°F.

Lay a sheet of aluminum foil on the open oven door to catch drips. Pull out the top rack, taking extreme care, as the rack is hot. Hang the hooks from rack, leaving at least 1 inch between the strips. Return rack to position, remove aluminum foil, and close oven door.

Meanwhile, heat the remaining marinade over medium-high heat until boiling. Reduce heat to medium and simmer for 5 minutes. Remove from heat.

A village on the upper Yangtze River

Roast the pork for 40 minutes, basting every 10 minutes with the marinade. Each time you baste, protect oven door with aluminum foil and check the water level in the pan. Replenish water to ½-inch depth as necessary. At the end of 40 minutes, the strips should be light brown. Turn oven up to 425°F. and roast for 10 to 15 minutes longer, or until pork has a sugar crust. Carefully remove pork from oven and set on a plate to cool. Serve warm or at room temperature. Slice ½-inch thick and serve as part of a multi-course meal.

Mu Shu Pork

One of the best-known dishes from Beijing, this simple stir-fry relies upon exotic ingredients ~ tree ears and lily buds ~ for texture and contrast. Another large part of the pleasure of this dish comes from wrapping the mu shu pork in mandarin pancakes, its traditional accompaniment.

½ cup tree ears

½ cup lily buds, about 40

1 tablespoon plus 2 tablespoons peanut oil

5 eggs, well beaten

1 pound boneless pork butt, trimmed

1 tablespoon plus 1 tablespoon soy sauce

1 tablespoon plus 1 tablespoon rice wine

2 teaspoons cornstarch

6 scallions, shredded

12 Mandarin Pancakes (p. 78)

¼ cup hoisin sauce

In separate bowls soak the tree ears and lily buds in 1 cup hot water each for 20 minutes, or until softened. Drain and squeeze dry both items. Discard tough ends of tree ears and chop into small pieces. Trim ends and halve lily buds.

Heat 1½ teaspoons of the oil in a wok over medium-high heat, add half the eggs, and cook for 2 to 3 minutes, tilting wok so that the eggs cover the pan in a sheet, to form a thin pan-cake. When bottom begins to brown and eggs are set, remove from wok and let cool. Add 1½ teaspoons oil to wok and cook remaining eggs in same manner. Cut egg pancakes into ¼- by 2-inch pieces. Slice the pork along the grain into ¼-inch-thick slices. Cut each slice across the grain into ¼-inch-thick shreds. In a bowl combine the pork, 1 tablespoon each soy and wine, and cornstarch.

Mu Shu Pork with Mandarin Pancakes, page 78

Clean out the wok and heat it over high heat until it just begins to smoke. Add 1 tablespoon oil and half the pork and stir-fry rapidly for 2 to 3 minutes, or until pork is no longer pink. Remove to a plate. Repeat with the remaining oil and pork.

Return the cooked pork to the wok with the tree ears, lily buds, and scallions, and stir-fry rapidly for 2 to 3 minutes, or until scallions appear limp. Add the egg shreds. Swirl in the remaining soy and wine and stir-fry rapidly until heated through and pork is cooked. Transfer to a platter and serve with pancakes and hoisin sauce. To serve, have each guest arrange about ⅓ cup filling on a pancake, top with hoisin sauce, and roll it up, folding in one side. Serves 4 to 6 as part of a multi-course meal.

甜酸咕嚕肉

S w e e t   a n d   S o u r   P o r k

The sweet and sour combination is indeed a favorite. A look at this recipe
reveals how few ingredients are actually needed to achieve the complex but
complementary results. The prudent amount of cornstarch used as a thickener
assures a wonderfully glossy, appropriately unsticky, sauce.

*1 pound boneless pork butt,
trimmed & cut into 1-inch
cubes*

2 tablespoons soy sauce

1 tablespoon rice wine

*¼ teaspoon plus 2 tablespoons
sugar*

¼ teaspoon ground white pepper

1 egg, beaten

*One 20-ounce can pineapple
chunks in juice, drained,
reserving ½ cup juice*

⅓ cup ketchup

⅓ cup distilled white vinegar

2 teaspoons cornstarch

*⅓ cup all-purpose flour mixed
with ⅓ cup cornstarch*

*¼ cup plus 1 tablespoon
vegetable oil*

*1 large green bell pepper, cut into
1-inch cubes*

3 slices ginger

In a bowl combine well the pork, soy, wine,
¼ teaspoon sugar, ground pepper, and egg. In
another bowl combine well the juice, ketchup,
vinegar, cornstarch, and remaining sugar.

Drain the pork from the marinade and
dredge lightly in the flour-cornstarch mixture.

Heat a wok over high heat until it just
begins to smoke. Add ¼ cup oil and half the
pork and fry, turning the pieces, until golden
brown on all sides. Remove with a slotted
spoon to a plate lined with paper towels to
drain. Repeat with remaining pork.

Carefully remove the oil and clean wok with paper towels. Heat wok over high heat and add 1 tablespoon oil. Add the bell pepper and ginger and stir-fry rapidly for 1 minute, or until fragrant. Add the pineapple and stir-fry rapidly for 1 minute. Restir the juice-cornstarch mixture and add to wok. Bring to a boil, stir-frying constantly. Add pork and stir-fry rapidly for 2 to 3 minutes, or until heated through and the sauce has thickened slightly. Serves 4 to 6 as part of a multi-course meal.

無錫排骨

W u x i   S p a r e r i b s

The spareribs that follow, from Wuxi in the east of China, rely on fermented red bean curd, a seasoning ingredient sold in jars, for resonance. Cured in brine with red rice vinegar and rice wine added, the fermented curd imparts an appealing spice-like flavor. The ribs are as tender as can be, braised as they are for one fragrant hour.

2 pounds pork spareribs

1 tablespoon plus 1 tablespoon peanut oil

1 tablespoon finely minced garlic

3 slices ginger

3 cakes fermented red bean curd

1 tablespoon soy sauce

2 teaspoons sugar

1 tablespoon red rice vinegar

1 cup Chicken Stock (p. 83)

Have the butcher cut each rack of spareribs across the bone into 1½-inch pieces. (You will then have three 14- to 16-inch-long strips.) With a meat cleaver, cut the spareribs between the bones into 4- or 5-rib pieces.

In large pot bring 8 cups of water to a boil over high heat. Add the spareribs and boil for 30 seconds. Remove, drain, and set aside. The spareribs will air-dry.

Heat a wok over medium-high heat until it just begins to smoke. Add 1 tablespoon oil and the garlic and ginger, and stir-fry rapidly for 30 seconds, or until fragrant. Add the remaining oil and the spareribs and cook 3 to 4 minutes, or until the spareribs are lightly browned. Add the bean curd, soy, sugar, and vinegar, and stir-fry rapidly, breaking up the bean curd with the back of a spoon, for 1 to 2 minutes, or until the spareribs are well coated. Add the stock and bring to a boil. Reduce the heat to low, and simmer covered, stirring occasionally, for 45 minutes to 1

hour, or until the spareribs are tender when pierced with a knife. Cut each piece into 2 or 3 ribs and serve with sauce. Serves 4 to 6 as part of a multi-course meal.

陳皮牛肉

Orange-Flavored Beef

Earlier in these pages we have seen how lemon in Chinese cooking combines with chicken; here another citrus ~ orange ~ combines with beef. The same principle, but everything else after that is entirely different, down to the method of preparation. There is absolutely no substitute for the dried peel here. Fresh will not do as it is not yet able to cast its spell and lend a subtle, rich, deep flavor specific to the dish.

3 strips orange or tangerine peel

¾ pound flank steak, trimmed

1 tablespoon soy sauce

1 tablespoon rice wine

1 tablespoon bean sauce

1 tablespoon plus 1 teaspoon cornstarch

3 tablespoons peanut oil

2 tablespoons Chicken Stock (p. 83)

2 teaspoons sugar

1 teaspoon white rice vinegar

1 tablespoon finely minced ginger

2 teaspoons finely minced garlic

1 large red bell pepper, cut into slivers ¼-inch thick by 2-inches long

¼ cup minced scallions

In a small bowl soak the peel in hot water for 15 minutes, or until softened. Drain and squeeze dry. Finely shred peel to make about 2 tablespoons.

Slice the steak along the grain into 2-inch-wide strips. Cut each strip across the grain into ¼-inch-thick slices. In a bowl combine well the beef, soy, wine, bean sauce, and 1 tablespoon cornstarch. Stir in 1 tablespoon oil.

In a bowl combine well the stock, sugar, vinegar, and remaining cornstarch.

Commune workers harvesting rice

Heat a wok over medium-high heat until it just begins to smoke. Add 1 tablespoon oil and the beef, spreading it in wok. Cook undisturbed for 1 to 2 minutes, letting meat begin to brown. Then stir-fry rapidly for 1 to 2 minutes, or until browned but still slightly rare. Remove to a plate.

Add 1 tablespoon oil to wok with the ginger, garlic, and peel. Stir-fry rapidly for 30 seconds, or until fragrant. Add the bell pepper and stir-fry rapidly for 1 minute, or until slightly softened. Add the beef and scallions and stir-fry rapidly for 1 minute.

Restir the cornstarch mixture and swirl it into wok. Stir-fry rapidly for 1 minute more, or until the beef is heated through and the sauce has thickened slightly. Serve immediately. Serves 4 to 6 as part of a multi-course meal.

湖南牛肉

Hunan-Style Chili Beef

Both Hunan and Sichuan provinces are known for their spicy combinations.
And while some like it hot, others do not. Should you fall in that last group,
by all means decrease the peppers in this recipe by half, and serve with Stir-Fried
Spinach with Fragrant Garlic (p. 56) as a way of cooling things off.

¾ pound flank steak, trimmed

1 tablespoon plus 2 tablespoons
   soy sauce

1 tablespoon rice wine

1 tablespoon cornstarch

3 tablespoons peanut oil

2 tablespoons fermented black
   beans

2 hot green chili peppers

2 hot red chili peppers

1 tablespoon finely minced
   ginger

1 tablespoon finely minced garlic

1 teaspoon red rice vinegar

1 teaspoon sesame oil

½ teaspoon sugar

Slice the steak along the grain into 2-inch-wide strips. Cut each strip across the grain into ¼-inch-thick slices. In a bowl combine well the beef, 1 tablespoon soy, wine, and cornstarch. Stir in 1 tablespoon peanut oil.

Rinse the beans in several changes of cold water and drain. Using the back of a cleaver, mash coarsely. Wearing plastic gloves, stem the chilis and remove the seeds. Slice chilis into ¼-inch-thick strips.

Heat a wok over medium-high heat until it just begins to smoke. Add 1 tablespoon peanut oil and beef, spreading it in wok. Cook undisturbed for 1 to 2 minutes, letting meat begin to brown. Then stir-fry rapidly for 1 to 2 minutes, or until browned but still slightly

Hunan-Style Chili Beef & Stir-Fried Spinach with Fragrant Garlic, page 56

rare. Remove to a plate. Add 1 tablespoon peanut oil to wok with the ginger, garlic, and beans. Stir-fry rapidly for 30 seconds, or until fragrant. Add the chilis and stir-fry rapidly for 1 minute, or until chilis are limp.

Add the beef and stir-fry rapidly for 1 more minute. Add the remaining soy, vinegar, sesame oil, and sugar and stir-fry rapidly until beef is heated through. Serve immediately. Serves 4 to 6 as part of a multi-course meal.

湖南羊肉
L a m b   w i t h   L e e k s

While one doesn't think immediately of lamb as being part of the Chinese
cooking repertoire, it has been used since ancient times, in the form of mutton,
and was particularly prized by Mongolian rulers when they took over China in the
thirteenth century. Today, lamb is eaten mostly in the north of China, where the
winters are long and cold, and hearty fare is imperative. The flavor of lamb
is offset here by the onion family ~ the leeks and garlic ~ and a bean sauce
combination. It is very important that the leeks be completely drained; otherwise
they will release water into the sauce, diluting its texture and taste.

½ pound leeks

*¾ pound boneless loin or
shoulder of lamb, trimmed*

1 tablespoon soy sauce

*1 tablespoon plus 1 tablespoon
rice wine*

1 tablespoon cornstarch

*½ teaspoon plus 1 teaspoon
Sichuan peppercorns, dry
roasted & ground*

2 teaspoons sesame oil

1 tablespoon hot bean sauce

1 tablespoon bean sauce

¼ teaspoon sugar

3 tablespoons peanut oil

4 garlic cloves, thinly sliced

Trim the leeks, removing the green part, and
cut the white part into fine shreds, about 2
inches long. Wash and drain thoroughly.

Cut the lamb across the grain into
¼-inch-thick slices, 2-inches long and
1½-inches wide. In a bowl combine well the
lamb, soy, 1 tablespoon wine, the cornstarch, and ½ teaspoon peppercorns. Stir in
the sesame oil. In another bowl combine
both bean sauces, the remaining wine and

Washing vegetables in the Li River

peppercorns, and the sugar.

Heat a wok over high heat until it just begins to smoke. Add 1 tablespoon peanut oil and the lamb, spreading it in wok. Cook, undisturbed for 1 to 2 minutes, letting meat begin to brown. Then stir-fry rapidly for 1 to 2 minutes, or until browned but still slightly rare. Remove to a plate.

Add 1 tablespoon oil to wok with the garlic and leeks. Stir-fry rapidly for 1 to 2 minutes, or until the leeks are slightly softened. Add the remaining oil and the lamb and stir-fry rapidly for 1 to 2 minutes, or until heated through. Swirl in the bean sauce mixture and stir-fry rapidly for 1 minute. Serves 4 to 6 as part of a multi-course meal.

清蒸全魚

Steamed Sea Bass

A wonderful way to enjoy the flavor of fresh-caught fish or shellfish is to steam it, as in this classic preparation from the southern and central coasts of China. The aromas are pure; the texture is moist; the presentation disarmingly honest. In this family-style dish, the whole fish is brought to the table, and diners use their chopsticks to remove portions. The tender cheeks of the fish are the most prized pieces, but by centuries-old custom, diners must wait until they are awarded by the head of the family to a family member.

One 1½- to 2-pound sea bass, cleaned & gutted, with head & tail intact

2 teaspoons kosher salt

3 Chinese dried mushrooms

2 teaspoons finely minced garlic

4 slices ginger, finely shredded

2 scallions, finely shredded

2 tablespoons soy sauce

1 tablespoon rice wine

¼ teaspoon sugar

1 tablespoon peanut oil

½ teaspoon sesame oil

Coriander sprigs for garnish

Thoroughly rinse the fish in cold water and pat dry. Sprinkle salt into the cavity and over the outside.

In a bowl soak the mushrooms in ½ cup hot water for 15 minutes, or until softened. Drain and squeeze dry. Cut off and discard stems, and slice the caps into fine shreds.

Put the fish on an oval heatproof plate with a rim. Evenly sprinkle the mushrooms, garlic, ginger, and scallions over fish. Drizzle the soy, wine, and sugar over the top. Arrange a rack in a wok and make sure that the plate can sit on the rack without touching the sides of wok. Remove plate and add 1 inch of water

to wok. Cover and bring to a boil over high heat. Uncover, place plate on rack, cover tightly, and steam for 13 to 15 minutes, or until the fish flakes when tested with a fork. Remove plate from wok.

Meanwhile, in a small skillet heat the peanut and sesame oil until almost smoking. Carefully pour the hot oil all over the fish. The oil will make a crackling sound as it hits the fish. Garnish with the coriander sprigs and serve immediately. Serves 4 to 6 as part of a multi-course meal.

乾煎蝦

D r y - F r i e d   S h r i m p

Shrimp are put to superb use in a variety of ways in Chinese cooking, and often the simpler the preparation, the better. Here the shrimp are "dry-fried," meaning fried with a minimum amount of oil and no sauce, then made fragrant with ginger, garlic, and scallions. Still in the shells, the shrimp turn a glistening orange in a matter of minutes. If you are eating these truly Chinese-style, no fingers are allowed. The mouth, teeth, and tongue, with a little help from your chopsticks, do the work.

1½ pounds medium shrimp

2 teaspoons plus 1 tablespoon peanut oil

1 tablespoon kosher salt

2 tablespoons finely minced ginger

2 tablespoons finely minced garlic

½ cup chopped scallions

½ teaspoon sugar

1 teaspoon Sichuan peppercorns, dry roasted & ground

2 tablespoons rice wine

Remove legs from the shrimp. Wash shrimp, drain, and pat dry with paper towels.

Heat a wok over high heat until it just begins to smoke. Add 2 teaspoons oil, salt, and shrimp and stir-fry rapidly for 2 to 3 minutes, or until slightly orange. (The wok will be slightly "dry" with the minimal amount of oil, but with continual stir-frying shrimp and salt will not stick in a seasoned wok.) Add the remaining oil, the ginger, garlic, and scallions and stir-fry rapidly for 2 minutes, or until shells begin to brown lightly. Add the sugar, peppercorns, and wine and stir-fry rapidly for 1 minute, or until wine has evaporated and shrimp are just cooked through. Serves 4 to 6 as part of a multi-course meal.

雪豆炒干貝

Scallops with Vegetables and Spicy Sauce

This dish from the western part of China combines the Chinese red of peppers, the emerald green of snow peas, and the snowy rounds of scallops into a beautful whole. This is hot, but not fiery. For the courageous, add more chili paste and chili peppers.

1½ pounds sea scallops, washed & drained

1 tablespoon plus 1 tablespoon soy sauce

2 teaspoons plus 1 tablespoon rice wine

2 tablespoons plus 2 teaspoons cornstarch

½ teaspoon plus 2 teaspoons sugar

¼ cup Chicken Stock (p. 83)

2 teaspoons oyster sauce

1 teaspoon sesame oil

½ teaspoon chili paste

½ pound snow peas, strings removed

3 tablespoons plus 1 tablespoon peanut oil

4 whole dried red chili peppers

4 pieces dried orange peel

1 star anise

4 slices ginger

3 garlic cloves, smashed & peeled

4 scallions, cut into 2-inch sections

2 large red bell peppers, cut into 1-inch cubes

Halve or cut into thirds any large scallops so that all scallops are approximately the same size. In a bowl combine well the scallops, 1 tablespoon soy, 2 teaspoons wine, 2 tablespoons cornstarch, and ½ teaspoon sugar. Cover loosely with plastic wrap. In another bowl combine the stock, remaining soy, wine, cornstarch, and sugar, and the oyster sauce, sesame oil, and chili paste.

In a saucepan of lightly salted water

blanch the snow peas for 1 to 2 minutes, or until they turn bright green. Refresh under cold water and drain.

Heat 3 tablespoons peanut oil in a wok over high heat until it just begins to smoke. Reduce heat to medium high, carefully add the chili peppers, orange peel, and star anise, and cook for 1 to 2 minutes, or until the ingredients have charred. With a slotted spoon, carefully remove and discard.

Increase heat to high and add half the scallops. Stir-fry rapidly for 3 to 4 minutes, or until scallops are firm and slightly browned. Remove with slotted spoon to a plate. Repeat with remaining scallops. Without cleaning the wok, add 1 tablespoon peanut oil, ginger, garlic, scallions, and bell peppers. Stir-fry rapidly for 2 to 3 minutes, or until peppers begin to soften. Restir the stock mixture and swirl into wok. Add scallops and snow peas and stir-fry rapidly for 1 to 2 minutes, or until scallops are heated through and sauce has thickened slightly. Serves 4 to 6 as part of a multi-course meal.

豉汁炒蟹

Stir-Fried Crab in Black Bean Sauce

The Chinese believe that for the sweetest flavor, fish and shellfish should be killed as close to the time of cooking as possible. In this recipe from the bountiful southern coast of China, it is the marvelous sweetness of crab that is captured, and then enhanced, by a handful of basic Chinese ingredients.

One 2-pound Dungeness crab

2 tablespoons fermented black beans

2 tablespoons peanut oil

2 tablespoons finely shredded ginger

1 tablespoon finely minced garlic

1 cup plus 3 tablespoons Chicken Stock (p. 83)

2 tablespoons rice wine

1 tablespoon cornstarch

1 egg, lightly beaten

⅓ cup finely minced scallions

Have the fishmonger prepare the crab as close as possible to the time you are going to cook it. The fishmonger will remove and discard the main shell. The crab should be rinsed well in cold water and the main body cut into 4 pieces. The legs and claws should be cracked lightly.

Rinse the beans in several changes of cold water and drain. Using the back of a cleaver, mash coarsely.

Heat a wok over medium-high heat until it just begins to smoke. Add the oil, ginger, and garlic and stir-fry rapidly for 30 seconds, or until fragrant. Add the beans and crab pieces and stir-fry rapidly for 3 to 4 minutes, or until the shells begin to turn bright orange. Add 1 cup stock and bring to a boil. Add the wine and stir for 5 to 8 minutes, or until broth is reduced slightly.

Combine well the remaining stock and the

cornstarch. Swirl in the mixture and stir-fry rapidly until slightly thickened. Add the egg and scallions and stir-fry rapidly 1 minute, or until the egg is flowered or set in strands, and the scallions are bright green. Serve immediately. Serves 4 to 6 as part of a multi-course meal.

海鮮保

Seafood Hotpot

Hotpot cooking is one-pot cooking; ingredients simmer in the most flavorful of broths until done. The aim is for the sweetest flavors attainable, but aesthetics such as the arrangement and color of the ingredients in the pot are also important. Sand pots are inexpensive and readily available, but a heavy, covered casserole for stovetop cooking is a substitute.

4 Chinese dried mushrooms

2 ounces bean thread noodles

1 small squid, about 2½ ounces, cleaned

6 cups shredded Napa cabbage

3 slices ginger

1 cup Chicken Stock (p. 83)

½ pound medium shrimp, shelled & deveined

½ pound sea scallops

1 cake firm tofu, about 8 ounces, rinsed & cut into ½-inch cubes

2 tablespoons finely shredded canned bamboo shoots, rinsed & drained

½ teaspoon sesame oil

¼ teaspoon ground white pepper

1 scallion, finely shredded

In a bowl soak the mushrooms in ½ cup hot water for 15 minutes, or until softened. Remove mushrooms, reserving the soaking liquid, and squeeze dry. Strain the liquid. Cut off and discard stems, and cut caps into fine shreds. In another bowl soak the bean threads in cold water to cover for 15 minutes, or until softened. Drain.

Score the inside of the squid pouch in a criss-cross pattern and cut into ¼-inch by 2-inch pieces. Reserve tentacles.

Arrange cabbage and ginger on the bottom of a 2-quart sand pot, available at Chinese cookware stores. Add the stock

and the reserved mushroom liquid.

In the pot, arrange in order the bean threads, shrimp, scallops, squid and tentacles, and tofu clockwise in mounds. Sprinkle the bamboo shoots, oil, pepper, scallion, and mushrooms over all.

Cover pot and set it over low heat for 10 minutes. (If using an electric stove use a flame tamer underneath pot.) Gradually increase heat to medium; after 8 to 10 minutes the liquid should begin to simmer. Uncover and gently stir ingredients to make sure everything cooks evenly. Cover and cook for 3 to 5 minutes, or until the seafood is cooked through. Serve immediately. Serves 4 to 6 as part of a multi-course meal.

干扁四季豆

Dry-Fried Longbeans with Pork

No one would suspect the medley of Chinese ingredients here ~ the dried shrimp, fermented black beans, chili paste, and Sichuan preserved vegetable (mustard green stems in chili paste and salt) ~ so balanced is this combination from the western province of Sichuan. Something wonderful happens to the beans' texture and taste from deep-frying that would not occur with any other method of preparation.

¼ cup Chinese dried shrimp

1¼ pounds Chinese longbeans, or string beans, trimmed & cut into 4-inch lengths

1 cup plus 2 tablespoons peanut oil

2 ounces ground pork butt

¼ cup minced scallions

1 tablespoon finely minced ginger

1 tablespoon finely minced garlic

1 tablespoon sesame oil

¼ cup Chicken Stock (p. 83)

1 tablespoon dark soy sauce

1 tablespoon fermented black beans

1 teaspoon red rice vinegar

1 teaspoon cornstarch

¾ teaspoon sugar

½ teaspoon chili paste

2 tablespoons Sichuan preserved vegetable, rinsed & minced

In a bowl soak the shrimp in ½ cup hot water for 15 minutes, or until softened. Drain and squeeze dry. Remove any grit and finely chop shrimp.

Wash the beans, drain well, and pat thoroughly dry with paper towels.

Heat 1 cup peanut oil in a wok over high heat to 375°F. With a slotted spoon, carefully add the beans and fry for 3 to 4 minutes, or until just slightly wrinkled. Remove wok

Rice fields in Yangshuo, Guangxi

from heat and transfer beans to a plate lined with paper towels to drain.

In a bowl combine the pork, scallions, ginger, garlic, and sesame oil. In another bowl combine the stock, soy, black beans, vinegar, cornstarch, sugar, and chili paste.

Carefully remove the oil and clean wok with paper towels. Heat wok over high heat until it just begins to smoke. Add 1 tablespoon peanut oil and the pork mixture and stir-fry rapidly until pork is no longer pink. Add the preserved vegetable and shrimp and stir-fry rapidly for 1 minute. Add 1 tablespoon peanut oil and the beans and stir-fry rapidly for 2 to 3 minutes, or until beans are heated through.

Restir the stock mixture and swirl into wok. Stir-fry rapidly for 1 minute, or until the beans are lightly coated with sauce and sauce has thickened slightly. Serves 4 to 6 as part of a multi-course meal.

香菇炒白菜心

Stir-Fried Bok Choy Hearts with Chinese Mushrooms and Bamboo Shoots

Bok choy, also called Chinese white cabbage, can be identified by its long fleshy white stems and mid-sized green leaves. While the small, young head of cabbage is favored, it is the heart that is most prized for its tender texture. Here bok choy hearts are quickly combined with another extremely popular Chinese ingredient ~ dried mushrooms. Fresh mushrooms cannot be substituted.

16 Chinese dried mushrooms

2 pounds bok choy hearts, washed & drained

2 medium fresh bamboo shoots, about ¾ pound, or one 8-ounce can, rinsed & drained

2 tablespoons Chicken Stock (p. 83)

2 tablespoons oyster sauce

1 tablespoon soy sauce

2 teaspoons cornstarch

1 teaspoon sugar

1 teaspoon sesame oil

2 to 3 tablespoons peanut oil

3 ginger slices

1 tablespoon finely minced garlic

In a bowl soak the mushrooms in 1½ cups hot water, stirring occasionally, for 15 minutes, or until softened. Remove mushrooms, reserving the soaking liquid, and squeeze dry. Strain the liquid. Cut off and discard the stems, and set caps aside.

Trim the base of each stalk of bok choy and peel off any tough skin. Halve or quarter each stalk and cut each leaf and stalk into 2-inch pieces. Halve and cut the bamboo shoots into ¼-inch slices.

In a bowl combine the stock, oyster sauce, soy, cornstarch, sugar, sesame oil, and ¼ cup of the reserved mushroom liquid.

Heat a wok over high heat until it just begins to smoke. Add 1 tablespoon peanut oil and the ginger and stir-fry rapidly for 10 seconds, or until ginger is fragrant. Add 1 tablespoon peanut oil, bok choy, and garlic and stir-fry rapidly for 1 to 2 minutes, or until leaves are just limp. Add the mushrooms and bamboo shoots and stir-fry rapidly for 2 to 3 minutes, or until bok choy is bright green and stalks appear slightly limp. (If wok is too dry, add 1 tablespoon more oil.) Restir the stock mixture and swirl into wok. Stir-fry rapidly for 1 to 2 minutes, until vegetables are lightly coated with the sauce and sauce has thickened slightly. Serves 4 to 6 as part of a multi-course meal.

麻婆豆腐

S p i c y   B e a n   C u r d

Although one would assume that the bean curd in this spicy stir-fry predominates, it is the tree ears and pork that star in texture, with the curd acting more as a custardy conveyor of all the lively flavors. Indeed this healthful, protein-rich combination from Sichuan is hot, but not incendiary, and is wonderful accompanied by rice.

¼ cup tree ears

½ pound ground pork butt

1 tablespoon plus 3 tablespoons soy sauce

2 teaspoons rice wine

2 teaspoons sesame oil

1 tablespoon plus 2 tablespoons finely minced ginger

½ cup water

1 tablespoon cornstarch

1 tablespoon peanut oil

2 tablespoons finely minced garlic

2 teaspoons chili paste

2 cakes firm tofu, about 1 pound, rinsed & cut into ½-inch cubes

½ cup finely minced scallions

2 teaspoons sugar

½ teaspoon Sichuan peppercorns, dry roasted & ground

In a bowl soak the tree ears in 1 cup hot water for 20 minutes, or until softened. Drain and squeeze dry. Discard any tough ends and chop into small pieces.

In a bowl combine well the pork, 1 tablespoon soy, wine, sesame oil, and 1 tablespoon ginger. In another bowl combine the water, remaining soy, and cornstarch.

Heat a wok over high heat until it just begins to smoke. Add the peanut oil, remaining ginger, and garlic and stir-fry rapidly for 30 seconds, or until fragrant. Add the chili paste and tree ears and stir-fry rapidly for 30 seconds. Add the pork mixture and stir-fry

rapidly for 2 minutes, or until pork is no longer pink. Add the tofu, scallions, and sugar and stir-fry rapidly for 1 to 2 minutes, or until mixture is heated through.

Restir the soy-cornstarch mixture and swirl into wok. Stir-fry rapidly about 1 minute, or until sauce has thickened slightly. Stir in the peppercorns and serve immediately. Serves 4 to 6 as part of a multi-course meal.

羅漢齋

Buddha's Delight

Buddha's Delight is among the most popular vegetarian combinations in China. The number of ingredients can range from ten to eighteen in the variations of this dish. The cabbage must be well drained, or it will give off too much moisture in the wok.

Four 8-inch pieces dried bean curd sticks

One 3 ½-ounce package bean thread noodles

¼ cup black moss or hair vegetable, if desired

10 Chinese dried mushrooms

¼ cup tree ears

¼ cup lily buds, about 20

1 teaspoon plus 3 tablespoons peanut oil

2 slices ginger

2 garlic cloves, smashed & peeled

4 cups finely shredded Napa cabbage, about ½ pound, washed & drained well

2 cakes red fermented bean curd

1 cup canned straw mushrooms, rinsed & drained

½ cup canned sliced bamboo shoots, rinsed & drained

2 tablespoons oyster sauce

1 teaspoon sesame oil

½ teaspoon sugar

In a large bowl soak the bean curd sticks in hot water for 1½ to 2 hours, or until softened. Drain and squeeze dry. Cut into 1½-inch long pieces.

In a bowl soak the bean threads in cold water to cover for 15 minutes, or until softened. In another bowl, soak the black moss, if using, in 1 teaspoon oil and cold water to cover for 15 minutes, or until softened. Drain both items.

In each of three separate bowls, soak the dried mushrooms in 2 cups hot water, and the tree ears and lily buds in 1 cup hot water for 15 minutes, or until softened. Drain and

squeeze dry all items, reserving the mushroom liquid. Strain. Cut off and discard mushroom stems and reserve caps. Discard tough ends of tree ears and chop into small pieces. Trim and halve lily buds.

Heat a wok over medium-high heat until it just begins to smoke. Add 1 tablespoon oil, the ginger and garlic, and stir-fry rapidly for 30 seconds, or until fragrant. Add 1 tablespoon oil and the cabbage and stir-fry rapidly 2 to 3 minutes, or until slightly limp. Remove to a plate. Add the remaining oil to wok with the dried mushrooms and stir-fry for 1 minute, or until heated through. Add the bean curd sticks, tree ears, lily buds, cabbage, fermented bean curd, straw mushrooms, bamboo shoots, and reserved mushroom liquid. Bring to a boil, stirring constantly and breaking up the fermented bean curd with the back of a spoon. Add the oyster sauce, sesame oil, sugar, bean threads, and black moss and bring to a boil. Cover, reduce heat to low, and simmer for 20 to 30 minutes. Check if there is enough liquid after 10 minutes and add up to 1 cup water, if necessary. Stir occasionally and when mushrooms and bean curd sticks are cooked through, remove from heat. Serves 4 to 6 as part of a multi-course meal.

蒜蓉炒菠菜

Stir-Fried Spinach with Fragrant Garlic

This quick vegetable stir-fry is particularly beautiful if you are able to find young spinach with its pink roots and tender stems still attached. Look for it in loose bunches in Chinese produce markets. Otherwise, use loose spinach, not the prepackaged variety, and remove the roots. Only three other ingredients contribute to the whole here ~ testimony to a very simple but aromatic combination popular throughout China. By the end of the cooking time, the garlic cloves may be slightly charred ~ another fragrance that adds to the overall pleasure.

*4 small bunches baby spinach
with pink roots, about
1 pound*

3 to 5 tablespoons vegetable oil

7 garlic cloves, smashed & peeled

1 teaspoon salt

1 teaspoon sugar

Wash the spinach carefully, but do not cut off pink roots or stems. Drain well.

Heat a wok over high heat until it just begins to smoke. Add 3 tablespoons oil and the garlic and cook for 1 minute, until golden brown. Add the spinach and stir-fry rapidly for 2 to 3 minutes, or until leaves begin to soften. Cover wok and cook over medium-high heat for 1 minute. Uncover, add the salt, sugar, and if necessary 2 tablespoons oil. Continue to stir-fry rapidly until limp. Serve immediately. Serves 4 to 6 as part of a multi-course meal.

白飯

Boiled Rice

There is no food more important to the Chinese than rice. While books could be written about how to prepare the most perfect bowl of Chinese rice, space here allows a few important pointers only: Although Westerners believe that washing rice rinses away all its nutrients, Chinese cooks wash their rice until the water runs clear. The amount of water that is used for cooking has been debated for centuries. A tried-and-true way to measure does not involve a measuring cup: Add enough water to cover the rice by ¾ inch, or to reach the cuticle of the middle finger when it rests gently on the surface of the rice. (Even though fingers differ in size, Chinese cooks swear by this method.) After the rice has boiled and the water has all but evaporated, the rice should look foamy, and little craters should appear on its surface. It is then, not before, that you cover the pot and lower the heat. After serving, if there is any leftover rice on the bottom of the pot, a crunchy treat can be made. Cook the pot over low heat for the duration of the meal and a crusty rice cake can be enjoyed afterwards.

2 cups long-grain rice

3½ cups water

Wash the rice in several changes of cold water until water is clear and not cloudy.

Spread the rice evenly in a 2-quart saucepan. Add enough water to measure ¾ inch above the surface of the rice, or pour in 3½ cups water. Bring water to a boil over medium-high heat and boil for 3 to 5 minutes, or until water almost completely evaporates, and rice looks foamy. Cover, reduce heat to low, and steam for 10 to 15 minutes, or until all of the water is absorbed and rice is cooked through. Turn off heat and let sit for 5 minutes before serving. Makes 6 cups. Serves 4 to 6 as part of a multi-course meal.

揚州炒飯

Yangzhou Fried Rice with Shrimp

When one thinks of Chinese cooking, the image that comes to mind is a last-minute preparation of the freshest ingredients, still steaming from the wok. Here is one of the rare occasions that uses a leftover, rice. This recipe from the eastern city of Yangzhou is deliciously quick and easy, and deservedly famous.

2 teaspoons plus 1 tablespoon peanut oil

2 eggs, lightly beaten

3 cups cooked long-grain rice, cooled & air dried

½ pound Roast Pork (p. 24), shredded

¼ pound baby shrimp, cooked

1 cup frozen peas, thawed

½ cup chopped scallions

2 teaspoons soy sauce

½ teaspoon ground white pepper

Heat a wok over medium-high heat until it is hot but not smoking. Add 2 teaspoons oil and the eggs and cook for 2 to 3 minutes, tilting the wok so that eggs cover the pan in a sheet, to form a thin pancake. When the bottom begins to brown and eggs are set, remove from wok, let cool, and cut into ¼- by 2-inch shreds.

Add the remaining oil and the rice to wok and stir-fry rapidly for 2 to 3 minutes, or until well coated. Add the pork, shrimp, peas, scallions, and egg shreds and stir-fry rapidly for 3 to 4 minutes, or until rice begins to brown. Add the soy and pepper and stir-fry rapidly to combine well. Serve immediately. Serves 4 to 6 as part of a multi-course meal.

鍋巴湯

S i z z l i n g   R i c e   S o u p

This extraordinary and dramatic dish from Sichuan combines the sweetness of
shellfish in a limpid clear stock to which a hot deep-fried rice crust is added. Upon
contact, the rice sizzles and hisses ~ culinary music. Timing is everything in making
this dish. If you prepare the shellfish in the stock too early, it will overcook,
and if the rice crust cools after being deep-fried it will not sizzle.

*1 recipe Boiled Rice (p. 57),
    cooked in an 8-inch saucepan*

6 Chinese dried mushrooms

4 cups Chicken Stock (p. 83)

*½ pound shrimp, shelled,
    deveined, & cut into ¼-
    inch cubes*

*¼ pound bay or sea scallops,
    cut into ¼-inch cubes*

*1 small cake firm tofu,
    about 4 ounces, cut into
    ¼-inch cubes*

2 tablespoons minced scallions

2 cups peanut oil

After the rice is cooked, remove the lid from
the saucepan and continue to cook rice over
medium-low heat for 15 minutes to absorb
moisture. Allow rice to cool completely,
uncovered, overnight if possible. Remove
top layer of rice and reserve for other uses, such
as fried rice. Only a thin layer of rice should
remain in the pan.

Heat the pan of rice over medium-low to
medium heat for 5 to 10 minutes, or until crust

on the bottom begins to turn light brown.
Once crust turns medium brown, begin to
separate crust from the sides of the pan with
a small metal spatula. From the time you heat
pan, the total cooking time can be 5 to 20
minutes. Try not to rush the process. Remove
crust from pan to a rack.

In a bowl soak the mushrooms in ½ cup hot
water for 15 minutes, or until softened.
Remove mushrooms, reserving the soaking

Stone sculptures in Dazu, Sichuan

liquid and squeeze dry. Strain soaking liquid. Cut off and discard stems.

In a large pot over medium-high heat bring the stock and reserved mushroom liquid to a boil. Add the shrimp, scallops, and tofu and reduce heat to low until ready to serve. Add the scallions.

Immediately, heat the oil in a wok over medium-high heat until it reaches 375°F. Carefully add the rice crust and fry for 30 seconds to 1 minute, until rice puffs. Trans-fer immediately to paper towels to drain, then break crust into pieces.

Quickly pour the soup into a tureen and transfer it and rice to the table. Drop rice crust into soup and let it sizzle. From the time rice is fried, it must be added to soup within 1 to 2 minutes, or there will be no sizzling sound. To facilitate the timing even more, add rice to the pot, eliminating the tureen. Ladle soup into bowls and serve immediately. Serves 4 to 6 as part of a multi-course meal.

鶏炒河粉

Chicken Chao Fun with Bean Sprouts

Noodles are so popular in China that entire small restaurants,
called noodle shops, are devoted solely to their preparation. Rice noodles
or *fun*, are particularly toothsome when stir-fried with tasty chicken
and crunchy bean sprouts.

1 pound boneless & skinless
    chicken breast

1 tablespoon plus 1 tablespoon
    soy sauce

1 tablespoon plus 1 tablespoon
    rice wine

1 tablespoon cornstarch

1 teaspoon sesame oil

2 tablespoons oyster sauce

1½ pounds fresh broad rice
    noodles

5 tablespoons peanut oil

8 cups bean sprouts, about 1
    pound, washed & drained

3 slices ginger

3 scallions, shredded

Slice the chicken across the grain into ¼-inch-thick slices. In a bowl combine well the chicken, 1 tablespoon each soy, wine, and cornstarch, and the sesame oil. In another bowl combine the oyster sauce and the remaining soy and wine. Separate noodles and cut into ½-inch-wide lengths.

Heat a wok over high heat until it just begins to smoke. Add 1 tablespoon of the peanut oil and the chicken and stir-fry rapidly for 2 to 3 minutes, or until chicken is just white. Remove to a plate.

Add 2 tablespoons peanut oil to the wok. Add the bean sprouts and stir-fry rapidly until lightly coated with oil. Add ginger and scallions and stir-fry rapidly until sprouts are just limp. Remove to the plate with chicken.

Add 2 tablespoons oil to wok with the

noodles, spreading them in the wok. Cook undisturbed for 1 minute, or until slightly crusty. Stir-fry rapidly for 1 to 2 minutes, or until light brown. Return chicken and bean sprout mixture to wok with oyster sauce mixture and stir-fry rapidly for 2 to 3 minutes, or until heated through. Serves 4 to 6 as part of a multi-course meal.

Sesame Noodles & Hot and Sour Soup, page 84

凉麵

Cold Sesame Noodles with Shredded Chicken

This classic combination is particularly popular in Shanghai and Sichuan. If using fresh noodles, know that they cook quickly and should be drained at once when done. Increase the amount of chili paste for more spiciness.

1 pound Chinese egg noodles, ⅛-inch thick

1 tablespoon plus 1 tablespoon sesame oil

One 1-inch piece ginger

2 garlic cloves, peeled

¼ cup Chinese sesame paste

¼ cup Chicken Stock (p. 83)

3 tablespoons soy sauce

2 teaspoons sugar

1 teaspoon white rice vinegar

½ to 1 teaspoon chili paste

¼ pound cooked chicken or Tea-Smoked Chicken (p. 18), shredded

½ cup julienned cucumber

½ cup bean sprouts, washed & drained

¼ cup minced scallions

In a large pot of boiling water, cook the noodles for 3 to 5 minutes, or until just done. Drain, rinse under cold water, and drain well again. In a large bowl, toss noodles with 1 tablespoon oil. Cover and refrigerate.

In a food processor finely chop the ginger and garlic. Add the sesame paste and stock, then pulse, scraping down the sides of the bowl, for 3 to 4 seconds, or until combined.

Add the soy, remaining oil, sugar, vinegar, and chili paste and pulse to combine.

Add half the sesame sauce to the noodles and toss to combine. Divide noodles among 4 bowls. Garnish each bowl with equal amounts of chicken, cucumber, and bean sprouts. Divide the remaining sauce among the bowls and sprinkle with the scallions. Serves 4 to 6 as part of a multi-course meal.

蝦仁撈麵

S h r i m p   L o   M e i n

There are a number of different kinds of lo mein—Chinese egg noodles stir-fried with meat, poultry, shellfish, or vegetables. Typically it is eaten at luncheon served with a stir-fried vegetable. This is noodle-shop fare at its best, very light and tasty.

8 Chinese dried mushrooms

¾ pound Chinese egg noodles, ⅛-inch thick

1 tablespoon sesame oil

2 tablespoons soy sauce

1 tablespoon oyster sauce

1 tablespoon rice wine

3 tablespoons peanut oil

2 slices ginger

½ pound small shrimp, shelled & deveined

4 stalks celery, shredded

½ cup thinly sliced canned bamboo shoots, rinsed & drained

In a bowl soak the mushrooms in 1 cup hot water for 15 minutes, or until softened. Drain and squeeze dry. Cut off and discard stems and cut caps into fine shreds.

In a large pot of boiling water, cook the noodles for 3 to 5 minutes, or until just done. Drain, rinse under cold water, and drain well again. In a large bowl, toss noodles with the sesame oil. Cover loosely. In another bowl combine well the soy, oyster sauce, and wine.

Heat a wok over high heat until it just begins to smoke. Add 1 tablespoon peanut oil, ginger, and shrimp and stir-fry rapidly for 2 to 3 minutes, or until shrimp begin to turn orange. Remove to a plate. Add 1 tablespoon peanut oil and the celery to wok and stir-fry rapidly until celery begins to soften. Add the remaining 1 tablespoon peanut oil and the noodles and stir-fry rapidly for 2 to

Fish trapping in Qiqihar

3 minutes, or until noodles are heated through. Add the bamboo shoots, mushrooms, and shrimp and swirl in the soy mixture. Stir-fry rapidly for 1 to 2 minutes, or until the mixture is heated through and shrimp are cooked. Serve immediately. Serves 4 to 6 as part of a multi-course meal.

雲 吞

Wonton Dumplings

Wonton dumplings are one of the quintessential Chinese snack foods.
This recipe shows how easy they are to make. Realize that we are taking no
shortcuts: The Chinese cook uses store-bought wonton wrappers, too. Look for the
refrigerated or frozen 3½-inch-square wrappers in Chinese markets.

6 Chinese dried mushrooms

10 ounces medium shrimp,
    shelled & deveined

6 ounces ground pork butt

¼ cup finely minced scallions

¼ cup finely minced water
    chestnuts

¼ cup finely chopped coriander

2 tablespoons soy sauce

1 tablespoon rice wine

2 teaspoons finely minced ginger

½ teaspoon freshly ground
    white pepper

One 12-ounce package wonton
    wrappers (about 80 skins)

In a bowl soak the mushrooms in ¾ cup hot water for 15 minutes, or until softened. Remove the mushrooms and squeeze dry. Cut off and discard stems, and finely chop caps. Strain and reserve liquid for Wonton Noodle Soup (p. 71), if desired.

Finely chop the shrimp to resemble the texture of the ground pork. In a bowl combine the shrimp, pork, scallions, water chestnuts, coriander, soy, wine, ginger, and pepper. Makes about 2 cups of filling.

Remove wrappers from package and cover loosely with a dampened cloth. With a point of a wrapper facing you, place a rounded teaspoon of the filling on the bottom corner. Cover the filling by rolling the bottom corner up until ¾ of the wrapper is rolled. Press the wrapper on both sides of the filling to seal

Fried Wonton Dumplings, page 70 & Wonton Noodle Soup, page 71

the filling in. Lightly brush a little water on one of the two side corners before bringing them together, overlapping the ends, and pressing them together to seal. Place the dumpling on a plate and lightly cover with a dampened cloth. Repeat with the remaining filling and wrappers. Makes 80 dumplings. The dumplings will keep 1 day covered and chilled in airtight plastic bags. To store, freeze dumplings spaced apart on a tray before transfering into airtight plastic bags. Dumplings will keep up to 4 weeks in a freezer.

炸雲吞

Fried Wonton Dumplings

Although deep-frying is much used as a cooking method in China, most Chinese do not typically eat fried wontons, preferring them simply in soups or boiled. Westerners, however, love them fried. And making your own sweet and sour sauce makes the dumplings all the more enjoyable.

½ cup pineapple juice
⅓ cup ketchup
¼ cup dark brown sugar
¼ cup distilled white vinegar

2 teaspoons cornstarch
2 cups peanut oil
20 uncooked Wonton Dumplings
(p. 68)

In a non-aluminum saucepan combine the juice, ketchup, sugar, vinegar, and cornstarch, whisking to make sure that the cornstarch is dissolved. Bring to a boil over medium-high heat and cook, stirring constantly, for 3 to 5 minutes, or until slightly thickened. Let cool. The sauce keeps, covered and chilled, for 3 to 4 days. Makes 1 cup Sweet and Sour Sauce.

Heat the oil in a wok over medium-high heat to 375°F. With a slotted spoon, carefully add half the dumplings and fry for 1 to 2 minutes, turning them over if necessary, or until golden brown. Remove dumplings to a plate lined with paper towels to drain. Repeat with remaining dumplings. Serve immediately with the sweet and sour sauce. Serves 4 to 6 as part of a multi-course meal.

雲吞湯麵

Wonton Noodle Soup

This soup is the equivalent of Chinese fast food, and you will be able to find some version of it in a noodle shop or at a fast-food stall in any Chinatown. It is nutritious and satisfying, and is always a dumpling and very thin fresh egg noodle combination. (The noodles are actually called wonton noodles in Chinese markets.) The better the broth, of course, the better the overall effect.

1 quart Chicken Stock (p. 83)

2 slices ginger

¾ cup reserved mushroom liquid from Wonton Dumplings (p. 68), if desired

40 uncooked Wonton Dumplings (p. 68)

¾ pound fresh wonton thin egg noodles

¼ cup minced scallions

1 teaspoon sesame oil

Coriander sprigs for garnish

In a large pot bring 1 quart water to a boil for cooking the dumplings and noodles.

Meanwhile, in a separate pot over medium-high heat bring the stock, ginger, and mushroom liquid, if using, to a boil. Cover, reduce heat to low, and simmer while the wontons cook.

When water boils, add wonton dumplings to the pot and return water to a boil. Add ½ cup cold water and the noodles and return water to a boil. Cook about 3 to 4 minutes, until the dumplings float to the surface. Drain well in a colander and divide dumplings and noodles among 4 large soup bowls. Add stock mixture, scallions, and ¼ teaspoon sesame oil to each serving. Garnish with coriander. Serves 4 generously.

葱油餅

S c a l l i o n   P a n c a k e s

A dough is made, a cylinder is formed, the cylinder is shaped into a coil, which is then flattened and fried. The result is the most sensational fried bread you may ever taste and, not surprisingly, a favorite street snack in China.

*2 cups all-purpose flour plus
about ¼ cup for kneading*

1 teaspoon sugar

⅔ cup boiling water

¼ to ⅓ cup cold water

2 teaspoons sesame oil

1 teaspoon kosher salt

½ cup finely minced scallions

½ cup peanut oil

In a large bowl combine the 2 cups flour and the sugar. Stir in the boiling water, and mix with chopsticks just until water is absorbed. Gradually stir in enough cold water so that a dough forms and pulls away from the sides of the bowl and is no longer sticky.

Turn the dough out onto a lightly floured surface and knead for 3 to 5 minutes, or until smooth and elastic. Cover loosely with a dampened cloth and let rest for 1 hour. Redust surface with flour and knead dough again for several minutes, or until smooth.

Divide dough into 4 equal pieces, and cover with dampened cloth. Using a floured rolling pin, roll one piece of dough into a 6- to 7-inch round. Lightly brush with sesame oil. Evenly scatter some salt and scallions on the round, then roll up into a tight cylinder. Coil cylinder around itself, into a spiral, and pinch the end under into the dough. Repeat with the remaining dough pieces. Cover coils with a dampened cloth and let rest 15 to 20 minutes.

Using a floured rolling pin, roll the coiled

dough on a floured surface into 6- to 7-inch rounds.

Heat the peanut oil in a wok or heavy skillet over medium-high heat to 375°F. Carefully add a pancake and fry 1 to 2 minutes per side, or until golden. As each pancake fries, press the center lightly with a metal spatula to insure that it is cooked. Remove to a plate lined with paper towels to drain. Repeat with remaining pancakes. Cut each pancake into 6 to 8 wedges. Serve immediately. Serves 4 to 6 as part of a multi-course meal.

蒸叉燒飽

Steamed Roast Pork Buns

To many Chinese children, these buns are one of the snacks they live for, with their slightly sweet pork filling and lovely, round shape. (Moreover, no chopsticks are required!) To grown-ups, Chinese or not, these are one of the classic dim sum selections, to be served for breakfast or brunch. Allow a minimum of three hours to make these at home and present them, for best effect, in the bamboo steamer, one of the most efficient, and beautiful, of all cooking utensils.

1 package active dry yeast

¼ cup plus ½ cup warm water (110°F.)

4 cups enriched bread flour plus about ½ cup for kneading

¼ cup warm milk (110°F.)

½ cup sugar

¼ cup vegetable shortening

½ pound Roast Pork (p. 24), diced

¼ cup plus ¼ cup Chicken Stock (p. 83)

⅓ cup minced scallions

1 teaspoon soy sauce

1 tablespoon oyster sauce

¾ teaspoon sugar

1 tablespoon cornstarch

In a small bowl dissolve the yeast in ¼ cup of the warm water for about 5 minutes, or just until it begins to bubble. In a large bowl add the flour and make a well in the center. Add the proofed yeast, remaining warm water, milk, sugar, and shortening. Stir with chopsticks to combine until a dough forms and is no longer sticky. Turn dough out onto a lightly floured surface and knead for 5 to 8 minutes, or until smooth and elastic.

Transfer dough to a clean bowl and cover with a dampened cloth. Let rest in a warm, draft-free place for about 2 hours, or until doubled in bulk.

In a saucepan combine the pork, ¼ cup stock, scallions, soy, oyster sauce, and sugar and bring to a boil over medium-high heat. Meanwhile, in a bowl combine well the cornstarch with remaining stock. When stock mixture comes to a boil, stir in cornstarch mixture and cook, stirring, about 1 to 2 minutes, or until slightly thickened. Cover loosely, let cool, and refrigerate. Makes about 2 cups filling.

Punch down the dough, then turn it out onto a lightly floured surface and knead for 2 to 3 minutes, or until smooth. Divide dough into 16 equal pieces, about 2 ounces each. Roll each piece into a ball and flatten into a 4½- to 5-inch round. Place 2 tablespoons of the filling in the center, gather the edges around filling, and pinch the top together. Turn the bun over and place on a 2-inch square of waxed paper. Cover with a dampened cloth. Repeat with remaining dough and filling. Let rise about 25 to 30 minutes, or until almost doubled.

Place as many of the risen buns in a bamboo steamer as can comfortably fit, leaving at least 1½ inches between the buns. Cut a ½-inch cross on each bun so that the buns can open slightly as they steam. Cover steamer with bamboo lid. Bring about 3 cups water to a boil in a covered wok. Place covered steamer in wok, and steam for 10 to 15 minutes, or until buns are almost doubled in size and are cooked through. Check the water level after 5 minutes and replenish, if necessary. Serve immediately. Repeat steaming process with remaining buns. Makes 16 buns.

春卷

S p r i n g   R o l l s

In China, spring rolls are traditionally served on New Year's Eve to celebrate the
end of winter and the arrival of spring. Because of their appearance, like that of
gold bars, once used as money in China, spring rolls also suggest prosperity.
The 7-inch square or round wrappers can be found in the
refrigerators or freezers of Chinese markets.

3 Chinese dried mushrooms

1 tablespoon peanut oil

½ pound Roast Pork (p. 24), finely shredded

1 cup finely shredded Napa cabbage, about 1 leaf

1 cup bean sprouts, washed & drained

1 celery stalk, finely shredded

¼ cup finely minced scallions

½ cup finely shredded canned bamboo shoots, rinsed & drained

1 teaspoon soy sauce

¼ teaspoon ground white pepper

One 4-ounce package spring roll wrappers (10 to 12 sheets)

1 tablespoon flour mixed with 4 teaspoons water

4 cups peanut oil

Sweet and Sour Sauce (p. 70)

In a small bowl soak the mushrooms in ½ cup hot water for 15 minutes, or until softened. Drain and squeeze mushrooms dry. Cut off and discard stems and cut caps into fine shreds.

Heat a wok over high heat until it just begins to smoke. Add the oil, pork, cabbage, bean sprouts, celery, scallions, bamboo shoots, and mushrooms and stir-fry rapidly for 2 to 3 minutes, or until cabbage and celery are just limp. Add the soy and pepper and remove wok from heat. Transfer filling

to a large bowl, cover with plastic wrap, and let cool. Makes about 3 cups of filling.

On a work surface, cover stacked wrappers with a dampened cloth. Start with one wrapper with the tip facing you and place about ¼ cup filling near the bottom tip, spreading it into a 2- by ¾-inch rectangle. Fold bottom tip up and over the filling, covering it. Fold in the sides and roll wrapper up tightly to form a compact cylinder. Paint far tip lightly with the flour paste and press down to seal. Place seam-side-down under the dampened cloth. Repeat with remaining filling and wrappers.

Heat the peanut oil in wok over high heat to 375°F. With a slotted spoon, carefully add 3 or 4 spring rolls and fry for about 2 minutes, or until golden. Remove to a plate lined with paper towels to drain. Serve immediately with sweet and sour sauce. Makes 10 to 12 spring rolls.

薄餅

Mandarin Pancakes

You may have to practice making mandarin pancakes, the traditional accompaniment to Mu Shu Pork (p. 26), before you perfect them. Roll these pancakes paper-thin ~ some say you should be able to see the filling through them ~ then cook them briskly until done but still soft. They can turn from pliable to hard in a matter of seconds. Practice does make perfect, though; and they can be made in advance.

*2 cups all-purpose flour plus
about ¼ cup for kneading*

⅔ cup boiling water

¼ cup to ⅓ cup cold water

1 tablespoon sesame oil

In a bowl combine the 2 cups flour and the boiling water, and mix with chopsticks until water is absorbed. Gradually stir in enough cold water so that a dough forms and pulls away from the sides of the bowl and is no longer sticky.

Turn the dough out onto a lightly floured surface and knead for 3 to 5 minutes, or until just smooth and elastic. Cover loosely with dampened cloth and let rest for 1 hour.

Redust surface with flour and knead dough for 3 to 5 minutes, or until smooth. Roll

dough into a cylinder 18 inches long, and cut into 1½-inch pieces, or 12 equal pieces. Roll each piece into a ball and flatten into a 2-inch round. Lightly brush one side of each round with oil, then press oiled sides of 2 rounds together to form a total of 6 pairs.

Using a floured rolling pin, roll each pair on a lightly floured surface into a paper-thin 7- to 8-inch round.

Heat a dry wok or cast-iron skillet over medium heat, add 1 double pancake, and cook about 1 minute, or until bottom is slightly

A fruit barge in Suzhou

blistered and center begins to puff. Turn and cook on the other side. Do not let pancake brown too much or it will harden; the pancake should be soft and pliable. Remove pancake, let cool about 1 minute, and carefully peel pancakes apart. Let cool. (If pancakes stick, use the tip of a paring knife to separate them.) If using immediately, cover pancakes with a dampened cloth.

Repeat with remaining pancakes. After 3 or 4 have been cooked, the wok may need to be wiped with a lightly oiled paper towel to remove any flour. If flour is not removed, pancakes may burn.

To store, stack the cooled pancakes between sheets of waxed paper. Refrigerated in an airtight plastic bag, pancakes will keep for several days. If using pancakes to serve with mu shu pork, steam the cooled or refrigerated pancakes in overlapping layers in a bamboo steamer for about 2 to 3 minutes. Makes 12 pancakes.

鍋貼

Beijing Dumplings

A perfectly made Beijing dumpling should enclose about one teaspoon of broth, created by the juices of the meat, vegetables, and stock, that bursts forth at the first bite. In fact, these delicious dumplings are usually served with Chinese spoons to catch that precious broth. Be careful when removing the cooked dumplings ~ you do not want to puncture them.

8 cups finely shredded Napa cabbage, about 1 small head

2 tablespoons kosher salt

2 cups all-purpose flour plus about ⅓ cup for kneading

1 cup hot tap water

½ pound ground pork butt

⅓ cup finely minced scallions

2 tablespoons finely minced ginger

1 tablespoon sesame oil

1 tablespoon peanut oil

¼ cup Chicken Stock (p. 83)

2 to 8 large Napa cabbage leaves for steamed dumplings

1 to 4 tablespoons peanut oil for fried dumplings

1 to 4 cups Chicken Stock (p. 83) for boiled dumplings

¼ to ½ cup red rice vinegar combined with 2 to 4 tablespoons finely shredded ginger for dipping

Coriander sprigs or chopped scallions for garnish

In a colander toss the cabbage with salt and drain well, squeezing dry to release moisture from cabbage.

In a bowl combine the 2 cups flour and the hot water, and mix with chopsticks until the mixture begins to pull away from the sides of the bowl. Turn the dough out onto a lightly floured surface and knead until smooth, adding more flour if necessary, for 5 minutes. Cover loosely with a dampened cloth and let rest for 1 hour.

In a bowl combine well the pork, scallions, ginger, sesame and peanut oils, and stock, and cover with plastic wrap.

After the dough has rested, redust surface with flour and knead dough again for 5 minutes, or until smooth. Roll dough into a cylinder about 18 inches long and cut the cylinder into scant ¾-inch-thick pieces to make about 24 pieces. Cover with dampened cloth. Roll each piece into a ball. Flatten each ball and, using a floured rolling pin, roll into a 3½-inch round, rolling from the center to the sides, making the center slightly thicker and the edges slightly thinner. Cover with dampened cloth and repeat with remaining dough.

Squeeze excess moisture from the cabbage. (The cabbage should be reduced to about 1 cup by now.) Add cabbage to the pork mixture, stirring to combine. Place a rounded tablespoon of the filling in the center of each dough round. Fold dough in half to form a half-moon shape. Pinch the edges together to seal, pleating it and brushing a little water on dough to help it stick, if necessary. Dust each dumpling lightly with flour and cover with dampened cloth. Makes 24 dumplings that can be steamed, fried, or boiled.

Steamed dumplings: Line a bamboo steamer with 2 large cabbage leaves. Place about 6 dumplings, not touching, in the steamer and cover steamer with bamboo lid. Bring about 2 cups water to a boil in a covered wok. Place covered steamer in wok, and steam for 12 to 15 minutes. Carefully remove steamer from wok and serve dumplings immediately. Repeat with more dumplings if desired. Serve with vinegar and ginger dip.

Fried dumplings (pot stickers): Heat 1 tablespoon of peanut oil in a wok over medium-high heat and arrange 6 dumplings smooth side down in the pan. Fry for 1 minute or until golden brown. With wok lid in hand, carefully

add ½ cup water and immediately cover wok. Continue to fry for 3 to 5 minutes, or until nearly all the liquid has evaporated. Serve immediately. Repeat with more dumplings if desired. Serve with vinegar and ginger dip.

Boiled dumplings: Bring a large saucepan of water to a boil. Add 6 to 24 dumplings and boil for 3 to 4 minutes, or until they float to the surface. Remove with a slotted spoon to soup bowls and pour 1 to 4 cups heated chicken stock over them. Garnish with coriander and scallions.

鷄湯

C h i c k e n   S t o c k

Chicken stock used in Chinese cooking should be sparkling clear and aromatic. The technique for making it differs slightly from a classic European-made stock, but the end result is the same in clarity and intent, and is preferable over any canned or dehydrated alternative. Chicken sold in Chinatown ~ any Chinatown, no matter the country ~ comes with the feet still attached. The feet enrich the stock and, if possible, should be included. Traditionally a whole chicken is used, but a combination of carcasses, backs, and parts can be substituted. If you do use a whole chicken, there is no other alternative, alas, but to discard it after so many hours of cooking.

One 3½- to 4-pound roasting chicken

8 to 12 cups water

4 slices ginger, smashed

1 teaspoon kosher salt

3 scallions

3 to 4 drops sesame oil

Wash the chicken under cold water and remove any pockets of fat and blood. Put chicken in a large pot and add 8 to 12 cups water to cover. Bring water to a boil over medium-high heat, skimming the scum that rises to the surface. Adjust the heat so that the stock does not boil until the most of the scum has been removed.

Add the ginger, salt, and scallions and bring the water to a boil. Reduce heat to low and simmer covered for 4 to 5 hours. Strain the stock through a sieve into a bowl and let cool. Refrigerate and remove the fat that hardens on the surface. Stir in the sesame oil. Covered and chilled, the stock will keep for 3 to 5 days. Bring to a boil before using. Makes 2 to 3 quarts.

酸辣湯

Hot and Sour Soup

There is much more to any Chinese dish than what greets the eye, as beautiful as that might be. Take, for example, soup. It often constitutes the beverage of the meal; it is sometimes served with the other dishes, sometimes at the end. It can be light and broth-based, or thick and stewlike. Some Chinese soups even have medicinal uses. From the north of China, this Beijing combination combines numerous ingredients into a flavorful, textured whole.

4 Chinese dried mushrooms

⅓ cup tree ears

¼ cup lily buds, about 20

¼ pound boneless pork butt, trimmed

1 teaspoon soy sauce

1 teaspoon rice wine

½ cup plus 6 cups Chicken Stock (p. 83)

3 tablespoons white rice vinegar

¼ cup cornstarch

½ teaspoon ground white pepper

1 cake firm tofu, about 8 ounces, rinsed & cut into ¼-inch-thick by 1-inch-long shreds

½ cup shredded canned bamboo shoots, rinsed & drained

2 eggs, well beaten

⅓ cup minced scallions

1 tablespoon sesame oil

1 teaspoon sugar

In three separate bowls soak the mushrooms, tree ears, and lily buds in ½ cup hot water each for 15 minutes, or until softened. Drain and squeeze dry all items, reserving the mushroom liquid. Strain mushroom liquid. Cut off and discard the mushroom stems and shred the caps. Discard tough ends of tree ears and chop into small

The Summer Palace in Beijing

pieces. Trim ends and halve lily buds.

Slice the pork along the grain into ¼-inch-thick slices. Cut each slice across the grain into ¼-inch shreds. In a bowl combine the pork, soy, and wine. In another bowl combine the ½ cup stock, vinegar, and cornstarch.

In a large pot bring the remaining stock, reserved mushroom liquid, and pepper to a boil over high heat. Add the mushrooms, tree ears, lily buds, pork, tofu, and bamboo shoots and return to a boil over medium-high heat. Restir cornstarch mixture and stir into soup when it boils. Cook, stirring, until slightly thickened, for 1 to 2 minutes. Remove pot from heat and slowly add eggs, scallions, oil, and sugar, stirring until eggs have flowered, or cooked in strands. Serves 4 to 6 as part of a multi-course meal.

八寶冬瓜湯
W i n t e r   M e l o n   S o u p

Traditionally a ten-pound winter melon is cooked for banquets, but one that size can take up to three hours to cook. Look for a melon of about five pounds, keeping in mind that it will need to fit into a soufflé or heatproof dish, and that the dish will need to fit on a rack in a covered large pot. The melon should have no soft spots and, ideally, should be of a pleasing shape and color. The lotus seeds and lily bulbs, two traditional ingredients that may be more difficult to find, are believed to increase energy and prolong life. Diced water chestnuts and straw mushrooms can be used as alternatives, although for their symbolism alone it is worth trying to find the seeds and bulbs in Chinese markets. The Smithfield ham called for is also available in most larger Chinese markets, but Westphalian ham can be used as a substitute.

1 quart Chicken Stock (p. 83)

½ pound pork butt (with or without bone), trimmed

8 Chinese dried mushrooms

2 tablespoons dried lotus seeds

2 tablespoons dried lily bulbs

½ cup diced canned or fresh bamboo shoots, rinsed

One 5-pound whole winter melon or, for serving home-style, ½-pound wedge winter melon, rind removed & diced

¼ cup finely shredded Smithfield ham

½ cup diced Crispy Roast Duck (p. 21), also available at Chinese markets, if desired

In a large pot bring the stock to a boil over medium-high heat. Add the pork and return stock to a boil. Cover, reduce the heat to low, and simmer while preparing the mushrooms.

Meanwhile, soak the mushrooms in ¾ cup hot water for 15 minutes, or until softened. Remove mushrooms, reserving the soaking liquid, and squeeze dry. Strain liquid.

Cut off and discard stems, and dice caps into ¼-inch pieces.

Return stock to a boil and add mushroom liquid, mushrooms, lotus seeds, lily bulbs, and bamboo shoots. Reduce heat to low, and simmer covered for 45 minutes to 1 hour, or until lotus seeds and lily bulbs are tender. Remove and discard pork.

For a simpler, home-style approach, add the diced winter melon to the soup, and cook until tender. Add ham and duck and serve. For a traditional banquet presentation, while the soup is simmering, wash the 5-pound whole melon with a hard bristle brush under cold water to remove the white powdery coating on the outside. Cut a paper-thin slice from the bottom so that melon can sit upright in the pan. Place melon in the soufflé dish or heatproof dish and if it is a little too small for the dish, wedge a piece of ginger between melon and the side of the dish to keep melon upright.

Using a sharp knife, cut V shapes about 3 inches from the top of the melon all the way around to give a serrated finish. Lift the top off and reserve for later use. Remove the seeds and string pulp.

In a pot that will hold the melon, place a metal rack and bring 1 inch of water to a boil. Carefully ladle the hot soup into melon, leaving 1½ inches of space from the top. Carefully place melon on the rack, cover pot, and steam for 20 minutes. (If desired, steam melon lid in a separate pot for 10 to 15 minutes.) Check to see if melon is nearly tender by piercing it with a knife. If not done, continue steaming, checking every 10 minutes. When melon is nearly tender, add the duck, if using, and the ham and cover pot. Steam 10 to 15 minutes, or until melon is tender, replenishing water if necessary. At this point it is very important to check melon every 5 minutes to make sure the sides do not collapse.

Remove the pot from heat and carefully remove the melon in the dish from pot.

Cover with melon lid, if desired. Bring melon to the table and serve immediately, cutting melon flesh ¼ inch from the rind and combining it with soup. Serves 4 to 6 as part of a multi-course meal.

北京糖糊桃

Candied Walnuts

Walnuts are featured prominently in Chinese cooking, in both savory and sweet dishes, and even though we have grouped these candied ones with "desserts" they could well serve as an appetizer or as a snack at any time of day. They are magnificent in color, crunchy and sweet, and nothing short of addictive.

1 pound shelled walnut halves, about 4 cups

1 cup sugar
5 cups peanut oil

In a large pot of boiling water over high heat, boil the walnuts for 1 minute, uncovered. Remove, drain well, and immediately transfer to a large bowl. Add the sugar while nuts are still steaming. With a rubber spatula, stir walnuts continuously, allowing their heat to melt sugar. After about 1 minute, no grains of sugar should be visible; the walnuts should appear to be coated with a clear liquid.

Line a workspace with a 2-foot sheet of heavy-duty aluminum foil. Heat the oil in a wok over medium-high heat to 375°F. With a slotted spoon, carefully add the walnuts, spreading them in wok. Fry undisturbed for 2 minutes, letting the sugar "set." Then stir carefully with the spoon to ensure even browning. Check for color. Fry for an additional minute or two, until nuts are golden brown. Remove with spoon, draining oil back into wok, and distribute hot walnuts evenly across the foil. Keep walnuts from touching each other or they will harden and be difficult to break apart. Allow to cool completely. Using paper towels, rub cooled nuts to remove excess oil. Store in an airtight container for 1 week to 10 days. Serves 4 to 6 as a snack or dessert.

糖香蕉蘋果

Candied Apples and Bananas

You may see this extraordinary preparation from Beijing called glazed or "spun" apples and bananas, and sometimes only apples are used. Whatever the variation, slices of fruit are deep-fried to become crusted, candied in caramel, and then plunged into ice-cold water to set the caramel. The result is a crisp exterior encasing tender, hot, sweet fruit.

4 cups plus 2 tablespoons corn oil

⅔ cup all-purpose flour

1 egg

1 large banana, peeled & cut into ¾-inch slices

1 large red Delicious apple, cored but not peeled, cut into ¾-inch chunks

2 tablespoons sesame seeds

1 cup sugar

Heat 2 cups oil in a wok over medium-high heat to 375°F. As the oil heats, put the flour in a shallow bowl. Beat the egg lightly in another shallow bowl. Dredge the fruit lightly in the flour, dip in the egg, then redredge in the flour. With a slotted spoon, carefully add the fruit to the oil and fry for 1 to 2 minutes, or just until a light brown crust is formed. Remove to paper towels to drain. This first frying can be done several hours in advance of serving. Do not be concerned if the fruit wrinkles a bit.

In a medium heavy skillet over medium heat, toast sesame seeds 5 to 10 minutes, stirring frequently until golden brown.

Lightly oil a serving platter. In a 7- or 8-inch skillet combine 2 tablespoons oil and the sugar and heat over medium heat, stirring constantly for 5 to 10 minutes, or until the sugar dissolves and caramelizes. (The color should be a light golden brown.) Stir in the sesame seeds and reduce the heat to low to

keep the caramel liquid. Do not let the mixture sit too long or it will solidify. Immediately heat the remaining 2 cups oil in a wok over medium-high heat to 375°F. With a slotted spoon, carefully add the fruit and fry for 3 to 4 minutes, or until golden brown. Remove to a plate. With bamboo chopsticks dip a piece of fruit into the caramel to cover completely, then transfer to the oiled platter. Repeat with the remaining fruit, taking care as it is very hot.

Bring the platter to the table with a large bowl of iced water. Have guests use chopsticks to immediately dip the fruit into the water to harden the caramel into a crisp coating. Serves 4 to 6 as part of a multi-course meal.

Bamboo shoots: Available fresh and canned, this unique vegetable adds crispness and crunchiness to Chinese recipes. Drain and rinse canned shoots, and to store, keep submerged in water in the refrigerator.

Bean curd sticks, dried: One of the forms of bean curd available, dried bean curd sticks are pale yellow in color and about 8 inches long. They require soaking before use. Sold packed in bags, they will last several months if kept in an airtight container.

Bean sauce: Made from fermented soybeans mixed with water and flour, bean sauce, or paste, is also available spicy. Sold in jars, it will keep, covered, in the refrigerator for several months.

Black moss: Also called hair vegetable, or fat choy in Chinese, black moss is an algae that adds texture, as well as its symbolic meaning of prosperity, to dishes. Soak in water before use, and, if desired, add 1 teaspoon of vegetable oil to the water to help separate the fine black strands.

Chili paste: Made from soybeans and chili peppers, and sometimes with garlic, this brown condiment livens up sauces for many dishes with its hot personality. Sold in jars, chili paste should be stored in the refrigerator after opening.

Coriander: Also called Chinese parsley, this pungent, musty-flavored fresh herb, not to be confused with flat-leaf or curly parsley, is often used in Chinese cooking as a garnish or chopped in sauces. Washed, dried, then wrapped in a plastic bag, it will keep for several days in the refrigerator.

Fermented black beans: Also called salted black beans, these small black soybeans have been fermented with salt and spices and serve as a seasoning. Refrigerated in an airtight container, they will last indefinitely.

Ginger: Ginger is the quintessential Chinese flavoring. Its spicy, hot flavor and rich aroma spark stir-fries and soups, braised and smoked dishes, and more. It is used in both savory and sweet combinations; without it, the entire repertoire of Chinese cooking would not be the same. Thought to stimulate the appetite, fresh ginger is called a root but is actually a stem. It should be firm to the touch with tannish skin and you should be able to feel the moisture in it by its weight. Whether it is called for shredded or minced or sliced in recipes, fresh ginger is not peeled.

Hoisin sauce: This is a sweet brown sauce of soybeans, garlic, sugar, and spices that adds a richness in flavor and texture to any dish. Available in jars, hoisin sauce should be stored, covered, in the refrigerator. If it is canned, transfer it to a jar with a tight-fitting lid for storage.

Lily buds: Also called golden needles, these are actual dried tiger lily buds and are used in Chinese cooking for texture primarily, but also to lend a slightly acidic flavor. Dried, they must be soaked, then trimmed before use. Store in an airtight container.

Mushrooms, Chinese dried: Available in different sizes and colors, ranging from dark to light, Chinese dried mushrooms are a prized ingredient often used in soups, stir-fries, and stuffings. Depending upon quality, they can be moderately to prohibitively priced per pound. They require soaking before use, but unlike other soaking liquids for dried Chinese ingredients, mushroom soaking liquid can enhance stocks and soup-based preparations with its marvelous flavor.

Napa cabbage: This is the almost white, elongated head of cabbage with tightly furled and crinkly pale yellow leaves you see in Oriental markets and many supermarkets these days. Delicate in flavor, it is a main ingredient in such dishes as Seafood Hotpot (p. 46), where it underscores the subtlety of the simple broth.

Noodles, Chinese: Probably the second most important food in China, noodles come fresh and dried, flat and round. All are long. Many are still made by hand in a dizzying display of expertise as the cook stretches the dough by swinging it round and round in the air until it divides into thousands of strands.

Some noodles are made from wheat-flour-and-water dough, others from wheat-flour-and-egg dough, others from rice flour or ground mung beans. Fresh egg and rice noodles are available in a variety of widths in Oriental markets and even some supermarkets. If fresh egg noodles are not available, dried spaghettini or vermicelli are reasonable substitutes, although the texture is different.

Bean thread noodles, also called cellophane noodles, are made from ground mung beans, and are pale and transparent. They must be soaked first to be used in soups, which renders them slithery and particularly toothsome in texture. They can also be deep fried in their dried form.

Orange peel, dried: The dried peel of this fruit will contribute a smoky, citrus spiciness. Fresh peel is not a substitute, but the dried tangerine peel is a wonderful alternative.

Oyster sauce: Made from oysters that have been cooked in a soy-sauce combination, this well-known salty condiment, so important in Cantonese cooking, enriches many sauces. There are grades of oyster sauce and the more expensive it is, the better it is. Store, covered, in the refrigerator.

Rice vinegar: Two kinds of rice vinegars are called for in the recipes in this book. White rice vinegar is prized for its clean, sharp, and light taste. Red rice vinegar is sweet and is frequently used as an ingredient in dipping sauces for dumplings.

Rice wine: This by-product of glutinous rice reminds us again of the incredible prominence of rice as a provider in the Chinese diet. Rice wine is a lovely pale-yellow color and serves for both cooking and drinking. Of the many varieties, Shaoxing rice wine is the most famous. Neither Japanese sake nor mirin are substitutes; if need be, a dry sherry can be used. Keep at room temperature.

Sesame oil: This magnificent golden oil, heady and rich in flavor, is made from toasted and roasted sesame seeds. Rarely is it used for cooking, serving instead as a flavoring in marinades and sauces. Keep, covered, in the refrigerator.

Sesame paste: Not to be confused with the

Middle Eastern sesame paste called tahini, Chinese sesame paste is rich and deep-brown in color, and will usually have oil floating on the top. Store, covered, in the refrigerator.

Scallions: Also called spring or green onions, scallions are almost always used whole, both white and green parts, in Chinese cooking for flavor. Trim off bearded root end and any wilted green ends.

Shrimp, Chinese dried: Available in plastic packages, dried shrimp have a remarkably strong odor which completely dissipates following soaking in warm water. Softened, they are used in small amounts as a flavoring in a variety of dishes.

Sichuan peppercorns: These reddish-brown peppercorns, which resemble flowers just about to open and are, interestingly, hollow inside, are actually called pepper flowers in China. Not peppers at all, but of the citrus family, they are not spicy in flavor, and are usually roasted before use.

To roast, heat a wok over medium heat until hot. Add the peppercorns and stir-fry them for 3 to 5 minutes, until slightly darker in color. They burn easily, so be alert. Let cool, then grind fine in a peppermill or spice grinder and store in an airtight container.

Soy sauce: A primary ingredient in Chinese cooking, soy sauce is a mixture of soybeans, wheat, and water that is fermented, then left to age. In this book it is assumed that "regular" or "thin" soy sauce is used throughout. On the rare occasions when dark soy sauce is called for, we mean a slightly thicker soy sauce (but not "black," which has had molasses added to it). Store all soy sauce in the refrigerator.

Star anise: This star-shaped pod with eight points is reddish-brown in color and has the compelling flavor of licorice. Used in braised and slow-cooking dishes, the pods are often removed before serving. Available in plastic bags, star anise will keep indefinitely, wrapped airtight and kept in a cool, dry place.

Tofu: This derivative of the soybean, made from soymilk, is called bean curd in the Western world. Long a favorite food in China, dating back to, some think, 200 B.C., tofu is widely recognized for its remarkable nutritional value and for its adaptability when it comes to things culinary. It can be fried, braised, or stuffed. It adds texture and protein to cold and hot dishes alike. Sold in cakes that are firm or soft, both of which should be fully submerged in water, tofu is a staple in the Chinese diet.

Tree ears: These small dry fungi, also called cloud ears and wood ears, add very little to a combination in the way of taste, but a vast amount of texture and crunch. They also contribute their interesting irregular shape and lovely dark color. Before use, they must be soaked and trimmed.

Water chestnuts: Available fresh or canned, this opalescent, wonderfully crunchy vegetable is available fresh or canned. Fresh water chestnuts should be firm to the touch; they need to be peeled before slicing. Drain and rinse the canned variety before using.

WEIGHTS

OUNCES AND POUNDS	METRICS
¼ ounce	7 grams
⅓ ounce	10 grams
½ ounce	14 grams
1 ounce	28 grams
1¾ ounces	50 grams
2 ounces	57 grams
2⅔ ounces	75 grams
3 ounces	85 grams
3½ ounces	100 grams
4 ounces (¼ pound)	114 grams
6 ounces	170 grams
8 ounces (½ pound)	227 grams
9 ounces	250 grams
16 ounces (1 pound)	464 grams
1.1 pounds	500 grams
2.2 pounds	1,000 grams (1 kilogram)

TEMPERATURES

°F (FAHRENHEIT)	°C (CENTIGRADE OR CELSIUS)
32 (water freezes)	0
108-110 (warm)	42-43
140	60
203 (water simmers)	95
212 (water boils)	100
225 (very slow oven)	107.2
245	120
266	130
300 (slow oven)	149
350 (moderate oven)	177
375	191
400 (hot oven)	205
425	218
450	232
500 (very hot oven)	260

LIQUID MEASURES

tsp.: teaspoon
Tbs.: tablespoon

SPOONS AND CUPS	METRIC EQUIVALENTS
1 tsp.	5 milliliters (5 grams)
2 tsp.	10 milliliters (10 grams)
3 tsp. (1 Tbs.)	15 milliliters (15 grams)
3⅓ Tbs.	½ deciliter (50 milliliters)
¼ cup	59 milliliters
⅓ cup	1 deciliter less 1⅓ Tbs.

SPOONS AND CUPS	METRIC EQUIVALENTS
⅓ cup + 1 Tbs.	1 deciliter (100 milliliters)
1 cup	¼ liter less 1¼ Tbs.
1 cup + 1¼ Tbs.	¼ liter
2 cups	½ liter less 2½ Tbs.
2 cups + 2½ Tbs.	½ liter
4 cups	1 liter less 1 deciliter
4⅓ cups + 1 Tbs.	1 liter (1,000 milliliters)

INDEX